Sayonara Singapura

Sayonara Singapura

PARAPURAM JOSEPH JOHN

monsoonbooks

Published in 2016
by Monsoon Books

No.1 Duke of Windsor Suite, Burrough Court, Burrough
on the Hill, Leics. LE14 2QS, UK *and* 150 Orchard Road
#07-02, Singapore 238841

www.monsoonbooks.com.sg

Updated new edition.
First published in Australia in 2014 by Publish-Me!

ISBN (paperback): 978-981-4625-35-7
ISBN (ebook): 978-981-4625-36-4

Copyright©Estate of Parapuram Joseph John, 2014

The moral right of the author has been asserted.

All rights reserved. No part of this publication may be reproduced, stored in a retrieval system, or transmitted, in any form or by any means without the prior written permission of the publisher, nor be otherwise circulated in any form of binding or cover other than that in which it is published and without a similar condition being imposed on the subsequent purchaser.

Cover design by Cover Kitchen.

Cover photograph of Domei news agency party courtesy of the Estate of Parapuram Joseph John.
All inside photographs courtesy of the Estate of Parapuram Joseph John.

Printed in Great Britain by Clays Ltd, St Ives plc
18 17 16   1 2 3 4 5

Parapuram Joseph John would have wanted
to dedicate his work to his long-suffering wife,
Annie Catherine

Following the surrender of Singapore on February 15, 1942, with almost 100,000 Commonwealth and Empire troops taken prisoner by Japanese forces, Winston Churchill said it was 'the worst disaster and largest capitulation in British history'.

The Australians
They grouped together about their chief
And each looked at his mate
Ashamed to think that Australian men
Should meet such a bitter fate.
And black was the wrath in each hot heart
And savage oaths they swore
As they thought of how they had all been ditched
By 'impregnable' Singapore

Dame Mary Gilmore, Australian poet

Contents

PREFACE	13
Zero Night	17
The Tiger	28
Bicycle Blitzkrieg	35
The Last Ditch	42
Final Blunder	49
The Sunrise	59
The Tedium	68
Magic Lamp (1942)	77
Willing Slave	87
The First Murders	99
Lovely Penang	109
Eyewitness	118
On The Hill	130
'Challo Dilli!'	142
The World War	149
Death Railway	159
A Present	168
Survival	176
Prayer Censor	183
Mokusatsu	194
Sayonara	203
EPILOGUE	214
PHOTOS	217

Preface

Parapuram Joseph John[1], the author and my father, was editor of *The Malaya Tribune* in Singapore when the Pacific War broke out and Japanese troops invaded. He was compelled to work for Japan's Domei news agency on an 'or else' basis and thus had an inside view of the brutal three-and-a-half-year Japanese occupation of Malaya and Singapore. His work consisted of subediting, checking and approving translations of Tokyo newscasts for local outlets. He also produced 1,000 words of anti-British propaganda broadcast daily to British Indian troops confronting the Japanese in Assam. *Sayonara Singapura* is a first-hand account of those turbulent times.

My father passed away more than 30 years ago. By then he had lost hope that this manuscript (which he produced with the help of a hired typist and which he sent to me) would ever see the light of day. The manuscript sat at the bottom of a drawer in my study until the family started talking about making a new attempt

---

1 Traditionally in Kerala the family or house name comes first, followed by the father's name, then the person's because of the sequence in the spoken language, Malayalam. I made the switch for myself and my children to keep up with the changed environment.

to publish it.

My father was No. 2 of the English section of Domei in Singapore, the No. 1 of course being a Japanese officer. An irresistible perk was that he could support Subhas Chandra Bose and the Indian National Army he was raising, with Japan's assistance, to drive out the British from India. My father broadcast 3,000 words every Wednesday to British Indian troops telling them they were on the wrong side. These verbal assaults were useful to the Japanese because they were preparing to attack India, ostensibly to win independence for India.

The broadcasts were taped and kept at SEAC, Lord Mountbatten's South East Asia Command. In *Sayonara Singapura* my father writes about wanton killings and the daily struggle to find food. He was present in Blood Alley in Penang, invited along by his Domei superior, where he watched, mute and in utter shock, when a 'cleansing' took place. He explains why so many young men and women went into the jungle. After the war he was interviewed by British agents and given a full clearance. He returned to work on the *Tribune* but he suffered bouts of temporary amnesia that culminated in a devastating stroke. It ended his working life. All his contemporary peers have passed away and a new Malaysia and Singapore have emerged, free to take their place in the world order of things. *The tumult and the shouting dies, the Captains and the Kings depart*[2], but this is eyewitness testimony up close and personal of Malaysia's and

---

2 Rudyard Kipling (1865-1936). *Recessional*.

Singapore's traumatic experience. His No. 2 on the *Tribune* was the late Mr S. Rajaratnam, who went on to achieve great things in Singapore.

Joshua Parapuram
Sydney, Australia

Parapuram Joseph John

1

Zero Night

I WAS IN CHARGE of a morning newspaper in Singapore, sleepily okaying Page One when 17 Japanese Zero bombers shattered the night. It was December 8, 1941, and Japan was at war with Britain. Almost simultaneously she crippled the American naval base in Pearl Harbour – fruit of years of spy work. Thus the third and last Axis Power entered the arena on the side of Nazi Germany and Fascist Italy. The Axis was in the ascendancy[1].

Having been fed daily with optimistic stories from London that the talks being conducted on behalf of Japan by envoys Mr Sabura Kurusu and Admiral Kichisaburo Nomura[2] in Washington would be 'fruitful', we in Singapore hadn't an inkling that war with Japan was imminent. As usual, we had a plethora of 'priority'

---

[1] Even though three months earlier the RAF had decisively won the Battle of Britain air war.

[2] Admiral Nomura, 86, died in Tokyo in May 1964. The then U.S. Secretary of State, Mr Cordell Hull, said of a Japanese note Nomura and Kurusu handed over in Washington one hour after the Pearl Harbour raid: 'I have never seen a document more crowded with infamous falsehood and distortions, on a scale so huge that I have never imagined until today that any government on this planet was capable of uttering them.'

news bits both from Reuter and British Official Wireless early in December hinting that the Washington talks might lead to 'hitting the nail right on the head'. And, as Japan wished, now we were totally unprepared. In fact, Singapore was in dreamland when the bombing began.

About 2.30am that fateful Monday one of my night reporters dashed into the newsroom and astounded everybody with the remark: 'There's bombing at the naval base!' I shot back with apparent gravity that it might all be due to the bottle, not a battle. We were still laughing when a minute later the old building violently shook due to an explosion in the harbour. They *were* bombs and they were coming nearer. And we wondered why the ARP siren was silent. The presses stayed idle and all staff were asked to leave the building forthwith. Where to? We had only seen pictures of air raid shelters in London. Instinct brought us to roadside gutters in which we crouched and waited for the all-clear siren – which never came, the same silence as when the bombing began. The newspapers naturally kicked up a terrible row in the following days over how sleep becomes death if the Air Raid Precautions unit continued to be deaf. Nearly an hour and a half later we filed back into the newsroom as the bombers left our shores having unloaded their missiles. The Zeroes had hardly flown north with empty bomb bays, defying the few anti-aircraft (ack-ack) guns, when the entire population (including, I expect, the man with the siren key) streamed into the city's lungs (fields or *padang*s, as they are called in Malay). Bewildered, they stood around for a while, then went home. All was quiet, by and by.

Little did anyone know that Singapore was shortly to disappear on a 3½ years respite from selling rubber and tin to the world.

There were at the time two English-language morning papers in Singapore: *The Malaya Tribune*, of which I was editor, and the *Singapore Free Press*, owned by the then afternoon *Straits Times*. The Japanese didn't like either but were singularly furious with my paper, which was financed partly by overseas Chinese interests. We were bitterly anti-Japanese, particularly since 1937 when force of circumstances compelled Japan to fan out her armies from Manchuria – the Japanese called it Manchukuo – to central and south China against General Chiang Kai-shek's forces. It was again force of circumstances – the hunger for rubber, tin, oil, manganese, bauxite and other raw materials – that drove Japan to seize, in turn, Hong Kong, Malaya, Singapore, the old Dutch East Indies (now Indonesia) and the Philippines.

There was a tacit understanding among *Tribune* staff to put in bold Doric type anything savouring of weakness in Japanese strategy from as early as 1931 when they seized the entire prefecture of Manchuria. From the day I joined the *Tribune* in 1938 I thought the staff was so drilled as to overdo the anti-Japanese bit. In the circumstances, I thought it a miracle that the Japanese bombers left us alone that fateful night. From that day, too, I knew that Britain was unready, and that the days of the island-city were numbered, though Allied propaganda which we meekly banner-headlined told the aggressor daily to keep his ships in the creeks of disembarkation lest he might be benighted in Malayan jungles. We dutifully magnified the London voice a thousandfold but we also posed a thousand questions to Fort Canning and Government House, from the day Japanese forces landed at Kota Bharu and destroyed its million-dollar defences within 24 hours. Besides, we front-paged as was customary on the *Tribune*, two or three choice bits of Japanese atrocities in China. It was quite conceivable that Japanese agents would have given Tokyo the exact location of our printing press as well as a full list of our staff, from editor down to *tampi*s, or peons, whose heads would be lopped off in due course.

With daylight came confusion confounding everywhere. White, yellow and brown nabobs stormed shipping companies for passage anywhere. They did not care where the ships touched or how long the voyage took so long as their destination was in cable link with the Bank of England. Several hundred could only obtain bookings for the end of January or early February, and in the event most of them lost their lives when Japanese navy bombers cut the shipping lanes into ribbons. The Straits of Banka was a shambles.

An Australian (or Latin American?) danseuse who was billed to appear at a fashionable hotel every evening until December 20 called us that morning. 'Mr Editor, please put in a news item tomorrow saying Miss Sonata Caressa has not cancelled her Singapore engagements. Anyway, Japs or no Japs I'm open to engagement until the next ship sails Down Under!' On any other day I would certainly have mourned with Singapore society the imminent departure of this lithesome ballerina, but on this fateful day when Churchill and his Far Eastern advisers were weeping with the six million inhabitants of Malaya and Singapore over the unheralded invasion, I did not care a hoot for Sonata's career.

Each man unto himself! Instinct drove the upper classes to the waterfront which was seething with humanity of every hue. But those who swallowed the propaganda that the delicate, short-sighted Japanese would soon be taught a bitter lesson returned to their homes and optimistically carried out to the jot and tittle every ARP direction.

Barring the Malay Regiment, few in the services knew the detailed topography of the north where the Japanese first came into contact with British forces. They knew little beyond the fine asphalt roads. But for a few well-defended points on the mainland which the Japanese were forced to subdue by frontal attacks, the steamroller moved relentlessly southward. The entire mainland was occupied in seven weeks.

Even after the lapse of a quarter century, I still wonder what made the British, Australian, Indian and Malay forces in Malaya (1941 – 1942) appear so weak before the Japanese thrust. God willed it so, one might say. If they hadn't licked the dust of Singapore and cleaned the streets of garbage under the eyes of an Asian population, the British perhaps wouldn't have so early granted independence to India, Pakistan, Burma, Ceylon and the rest of the procession. Japan may reasonably be deemed to have struck the first nail in the coffin of British and Dutch imperialism in Asia – whether the Japanese designed it so or not.

Back at the *Tribune* editorial desk, our telephones had been ringing frantically from the time the Zeroes departed. Our

Managing Editor, Mr Edwin Maurice Glover[3], was one thirsting for news. I told him: 'We were all in the gutter about two hours. Anyway all's well with us, and machinery. We're not hit.' The *tuan besar* (big boss) hurried to us from his air-conditioned mansion in Holland Park, five miles from our office in Anson Road, almost on the southern seaboard. It was seven when he arrived and called for a proof of Page One. Not a word about the war. The nearest we could come to it was a brief report on the Washington talks. This, too, managed to add another storey to the mental mansion the people of Singapore and Malaya were conjuring up. It said: 'When the White House conference reassembles this afternoon it is expected a new formula will be arrived at to dissolve the differences with Japan.' I hang my head in shame that such a story got onto Page One that morning.

Mr Glover rang up Sir Shenton Thomas, Governor of the Straits Settlements and High Commissioner of the Federated Malay States – quite a mouthful – who was fortunately in the closet at the time. Within the few minutes' respite, Mr Glover managed to disabuse himself of the cockney tirade with which he meant to assail His Excellency. Not because war had broken out but because the newspapers were still in the dark although the Pacific war seemed to have broken out seven hours earlier. A minute later Sir Shenton's private secretary asked Mr Glover to contact GHQ. Our reporters had been shooting back and forth into the

---

3 Author of the 1946 bestseller, *In Seventy Days* (Muller: London).

GOC's office in Fort Canning for two hours when a communiqué was manufactured from local observation and issued to us about 9am. It said Japanese naval planes reconnoitred the island of Singapore about 2am and bombs were dropped at a few points of the city. There was a cursory remark at the fag end: 'Japanese also landed forces at Singora and Patani (southern Thailand) and at Kota Bharu (north-east Malaya). Fighting is in progress.' This was one of the few communiqués that did not mention the notorious 'mopping-up'; it had an honoured place in nearly all the latter-day communiqués issued by GOC Malaya. You heard of mopping-up in Alor Star, and almost the following day of enemy infiltration into Perak which once again was mopped-up. It went on for seventy days when the Japanese finally mopped-up British remnants in Singapore.

The GHQ communiqué was inserted as late news in 10-pt caps (large capital letters) on the front page. And the *Tribune* finally came off the press six hours late. We were sold out in an hour.

The night staff was tired but few could go to bed that day because each had his or her own problems – where to eat or sleep, was it the time to scuttle? And above all, what should one do with wife and children, if any, and dependents? For me the problems were considerably easy. I was at the time staying in a hotel just a hundred yards from the office. Hardly a week earlier I had returned after a three-month holiday in India, and my wife and children were still in India. One of the best things I ever did for myself was to bring with me to Singapore that December a younger brother, Jose. He, too, learned the bitter facts of war.

The widespread uneasiness followed by the scamper to get out of that nasty hole before it was bombed to extinction was soon dissipated when it was whispered in the evening that behemoths of the Royal Navy, the *Prince of Wales* and the *Repulse*, were 'with us till the end'. Bitter disenchantment gripped both the civilian population and the entire Allied fighting services in 36 hours.

The nucleus of the Royal Navy's Eastern command, the battleship *Prince of Wales* and the battle-cruiser *Repulse* with an escort of four destroyers[4] – had in fact arrived in Singapore a week before the Zero raid and were nestling in the Naval Base unscathed. Few in the city were at the time aware of the naval presence, but within 18 hours of the Japanese landing in the north, roughly 450 miles from Singapore, the floating fortresses and their escort ploughed north to give battle. And the unsinkable were sunk – in the South China Sea off the Kelantan coast about 175 miles from Singapore about 3pm on December 10, 1941. How?

The following December I met a Japanese rear-gunner who was in one of the first nine bombers that attacked the two capital ships. As soon as I mentioned the epic sea battle, he rose from his chair, turned north-east to Tokyo and bowed to *Tenno-Heika* (Emperor Hirohito). He pulled his chair closer and whispered in broken English: 'We took off from Phuquok airfield [in Indochina]

---

4 The four destroyers were the *Electra, Express, Vampire* and *Tenedos*.

and arrived over the target – the *Prince of Wales* and *Repulse* with three destroyers[5] drawn up in a triangle enclosing the two warships – about 12.45pm on December 10. We had a direct hit on the *Repulse*, with several near misses, and one of our nine planes crashed into sea.' This attack by bombers was followed by two raids by torpedo-carrying planes, crowned by the final *coup de grace* by a last unit of 10 bombers. The next morning Japanese planes flew over the spot and dropped a wreath for both the British seamen (830 officers and men) and 10 or so Japanese airmen who died in the battle.

Admiral Sir Tom Phillips, who had recently been elevated as Commander-in-Chief of the Eastern Fleet, believed that with fighter cover and the element of surprise he could smash the Japanese landings. His commanders and staff officers unanimously agreed that inactivity in Singapore was impossible in the circumstances and that the sudden raid, though hazardous, should be attempted. He went down with his ship while Capt. William Tennant, who commanded the *Repulse*, managed to save himself, seeing action elsewhere.

Two hours after the sinking, five minutes past four on December 10 to be exact, Tokyo made a formal announcement from Imperial Navy Headquarters that 'the third day of hostilities has resulted in the annihilation of the main strength of the British Far Eastern Fleet.'

---

5 The *Tenedos* was sent back to Singapore because of a mysterious fuel shortage. I have not yet seen an official explanation

The communiqué added: 'From the outbreak of hostilities the movements of the two British capital ships have been closely observed. Yesterday afternoon they were discovered by one of our submarines carrying out a reconnaissance in co-operation with naval surface ships and the Navy Air Force. At half past eleven this morning our submarines again confirmed the position of the British ships, off Kuantan on the east coast of Malaya. Without losing a moment the Naval Air Force entered into a dauntless and daring attack at about 12.45. The *Repulse* was seriously damaged by the first bombs dropped and shortly afterwards the *Prince of Wales* was hit and developed a heavy list to port. The *Repulse* sank first, and shortly after at ten minutes to three, the *Prince of Wales* blew up and sank.'

But Singapore in general remained oblivious. That night as usual I was editing the *Tribune*. About 2am we had a brief message from London saying '*Prince Wales Repulse* sunk rpt [repeat].' I couldn't believe my eyes. Without comment I showed the message to our chief sub, a Chinese gentleman, a third-generation Malayan. There were tears in his eyes. Then the full story came on the wires.

The ships had no air cover, despite the lessons of the Atlantic and Mediterranean sea battles. I recollect that the total number of British aircraft in northern Malaya at the opening of the war was 110. At the end of the first day only 50 were fit for operations. By the time the Japanese had captured three or four airfields in the north in the first week, practically the entire British squadron had either been destroyed or pulled back to Padang, Sumatra. Even if any were available to cover the two ships, they would have been shot out of the skies like flies by the far superior Japanese planes. With that naval disaster, British aircraft were fully withdrawn from the scene of hostilities.

The following morning we carried a brief report on the sinkings softened by tons of propaganda stuff from London. Soon the city was drugged back to its wonted somnolence, and the queues in front of the shipping companies melted away. Soothing words gushed out of London in an avalanche. 'Stay put!' And we in Singapore stayed put. What else could the poor Chinese – I mean the Overseas Chinese who had little to look up to in China – and poorer Indians do? Each man was soon back at his work place, tin mine, rubber estate or petty shop. The cabarets, cinemas and bars were crowded every night.

2

The Tiger

RIGHT FROM THE START of hostilities almost everything the resident army and its public relations office did or tactfully did not do hadn't quite hit the mark. The sequel was the inexorable and chaotic push-back of British forces across four hundred miles of rubber, paddy fields and not-so-impenetrable jungle in fifty-five days. On January 31 forward patrols of Japanese 25th Army, commanded by Lieut.-General Tomoyuki Yamashita[1] (who didn't mind being called *Tiger of Malaya*), pushed along to the water's edge and inspected the Singapore skyline from Johore Bahru, capital of the southern peninsular state of Johore. Yamashita's objective twinkled like a diamond almost under his nose. And on the seventh day after the Japanese landed on the island of Singapore, Lieut-General A.E. Percival, GOC Malaya, walked up to the Ford plant on a hill at the 7th mile, Bukit Timah Road, and capitulated lock, stock and barrel to the Japanese conqueror.

First Percival sent a party of high-ranking army officers with the Colonial Secretary, Hugh Fraser, and a Japanese-speaking

---

[1] Yamashita was executed by the War Crimes Commission in Manila in 1945. Percival died in hospital in London, aged 78.

interpreter, a Capt. Wild, to the Japanese GHQ. Sticking out of the back of the car were two flagpoles. One carried the Union Jack and the other a white flag, both furled. The party was not even allowed to enter the lair of the *Tiger,* who ordered: 'Send Percival here right now, or none of you whites will be in the land of the living within an hour!' The party in the car fled, and re-appeared at the Ford gate with Percival – in 20 minutes. Abandoning the car at the gate, they walked up the hill where the Japanese High Command was waiting. The Union Jack and the white flag were now fluttering in the breeze, and Percival himself handed to Yamashita the white flag of unconditional surrender at 8pm on Sunday, February 15, 1942, within seventy days of the Japanese landing in the north.

From about 4pm that day we were surprised at the strange stillness that prevailed over the city. Unexplained explosions had ceased while Jose and I sheltered under a staircase on the ground floor of a fifty-yard long, three-storey block of flats in Middle Road in the heart of the bustling city. About 6pm we heard an unusually long-drawn-out all-clear signal. The siren – it was back! – last wailed more than three days ago, and there had been intense, indiscriminate bombing and shelling of military targets as well as civilian areas. In the last three days of old Singapore – Friday, Saturday and Sunday, the day of Percival's capitulation – the exhausted British Army, beaten and demoralised, consisting of an odd medley of Englishmen, Highlanders, Aussies, Gurkhas with their inseparable *kukris* (their traditional battle knife), Sikhs down to Malayalees, and 'other ranks' drawn from every part of

India, was hurled back into the city proper. Every street had its fighting men.

The blame for indiscriminate bombing of civilian areas, therefore, does not squarely lie with the Japanese. Even so, I wonder what made the Japanese airmen repeatedly bomb the overcrowded tenements in Chinatown. Why were they so cruel and inhuman to Chinese non-combatants? It might have been tit for tat – the tat which Generalissimo Chiang Kai-shek had administered to Japanese hordes on the Chinese mainland in the five or six years before the Pacific war.

Sino–Japanese enmity, so long as it remained 'hot' until war's end in 1945, could hardly be comprehensible to an outsider. Even before the Manchuria invasion (which the Japanese would dismiss as the Manchukuo Incident, a staged event by Japanese troops for an excuse to launch the invasion) representatives of these two nations could hardly face each other on equal terms. China had long maintained that in the dim past, three or four thousand years ago, a Chinese desperado fleeing the wrath of the great Emperor of China, spotted the uninhabited islands of Japan. And, cohabiting with the monkeys found there in abundance, he fathered the Nippon-jin or Japanese people. So goes the story. Hardly surprising that the Japanese continued to sickle the necks of the 'Chinese malefactors' from the Manchurian Incident right up to Hiroshima and Nagasaki in August 1945.

For me the seventy days before the surrender were days of a different kind of agony. Get out or stay put? What were the alternatives? Did I have a choice?

Despite the propaganda holocaust from London, by the middle of December it became generally accepted that the Japanese meant business. Their first major obstacle was Kota Bahru, the northern gate of Malaya and the capital of Kelantan State. It was defended by the 8th Brigade, 9th Indian Division, which was almost decimated in battle. And, according to a Japanese account[2] the invader lost 320 men killed in action and 538 wounded in the Kota Bahru battle on December 8. Destruction of the coastal defences followed by the seizure of the nearby RAF airfield within a few hours of fighting marked the first Japanese blow at the Singapore Naval Base.

The Takumi Detachment of the Japanese 18th Division then moved south via Gong Kedah and Trengganu to Kuantan on the eastern seashore which they reached by the end of the month. Another detachment of the 18th Division called after Koba landed at Kota Bharu on December 28 and reached Kuantan on January 3. Simultaneously there was rapid advance on the western front. There were four main lines of attack on the western front – the Imperial Guards Division from Thailand, the 5th Division and 18th Division (via Singora) and the Ando Detachment (via Patani). Of these the 18th Division landed in Southern Thailand on January 23 and converged on Johore Bahru by the 31st. The other three which landed at midnight of December 8 quickly moved south, smashing the major Jitra defence line and capturing

---

[2] *Singapore: Japanese Version*, an English translation of Colonel Masanobu Tsuji's book in Nippon-go. He was Chief of Operations and Planning Staff, 25th Japanese Army.

one strong point after another.

Within a week after the Japanese forces struck at the northern boundary, that is, by December 15, every Westerner, whether of the fighting services or not, had fled Penang, reputed to be the 'north-western eye of the British colony'. Not a single shot had to be fired by the small Japanese contingent that entered this charming island town on December 19. Resident Europeans had ratted the island without a word to the Malays, Chinese and Indians – they were asked to leave the island by GHQ at the dead of night. Little wonder that Penang welcomed the Imperial Japanese Force as harbingers of the Greater East Asia Co-Prosperity Sphere. And the Japanese were overjoyed at the cordial welcome. They were almost made to forget the war as they relaxed in the clubhouse atop Penang Hill, 2,700 ft. above sea level. In my view Penang is one of the mos picturesque scenic spots in Asia, being not so glaring as Bali, Hong Kong or Kashmir, which figure prominently on the tourist's Asian itinerary.

The forces that broke through the northern border had been ordered to stop at the water's edge and assess the enemy's positions across the narrow Strait of Johore. The Japanese commander surveyed the scene and exclaimed: 'The enemy is not within sight.' He found the enemy a mile away, and immediately began to unroll the British Army lines until he could closely inspect the much-publicised works at the Singapore Naval Base, 'pawing the ground in its last moments,' as a Japanese writer put it.

After Jitra the major obstacle to the Japanese southward advance was crossing the Perak River – which they accomplished with miraculous ease. Ipoh, capital of Perak, was overrun shortly after Christmas; and Kuala Lumpur, capital of the Federated Malay States and now the capital of Malaysia, on January 11. In a few days the Takumi detachment branched off westward from Kuantan to connect with the 5th Division assault on Kajang. The reinforcement (the Koba detachment) that landed at Kota Bahru on Dec 28 reached Kuantan on the east coast on January 3, moved south subduing defenders in Endau and Mersing, and closed in on Kluang with the 5th Division.

The push on the west coast was facilitated by the Engineering Corps, variously described as 'magnificent' and 'clever' by observers at the time. When the 500-yard long Perak Bridge was demolished by the British it was expected that the Japanese would take at least three months to repair it. However, heavy tanks were rolling south over it within a week. A bicycle mechanic, whose left foot suffered major dislocation in the Patani landing on December 8, walked all the way to Singapore on crutches, working with the Engineers. There was steel in that man, for the Japanese as a whole believed with full commitment that they were pushing south not to conquer new countries but to librate Southeast Asia from Western imperialism The average Japanese soldier, sailor or airman was imbued with the mission to annihilate the white masters of down-trodden Asia and to establish the Co-prosperity Sphere.

Ten days after the war began there was some rush at British hotels in Singapore like the Raffles, Sea View and the Adelphi. The story, by and by, leaked out that Europeans had quietly fled Penang. From that day Singapore took under its wing huge numbers of people of all races, classes and nationalities, from Alor Star to Johore Bahru. Fashionable hotels ceased to be hotels; they degenerated into refugee camps as the Japanese drove into Johore Bahru in cars seized from the British and armed with every conceivable type of munitions left by the fleeing British Army. Yet few chose to leave Singapore when there was time to do so. Slogans like 'Singapore must stand; it SHALL stand' had their opiate effect. The end, when it came, was all too sudden.

3

Bicycle Blitzkrieg

ALL THE WORLD was dazzled by the invader's stratagems. Few could believe at the time that Japan had a tank detachment operating in the north. How could they have landed tanks at Patani or Kota Bharu, neither a harbour? Or, were they the forerunner of the amphibious tank? Until almost the capture of Kuala Lumpur in January few had returned to Singapore from the battlefront to testify to the presence of enemy tanks. But they made their presence felt subsequently in Tanjong Malim, Kajang, Gemas, Kluang and points south. The defenders had nothing bigger than Bren-gun-carriers to match the Japanese tank which smashed through practically everything it encountered in the race to Singapore. And the Japanese 25th Army was outnumbered two to one.

The absence of Buffalo fighters from Malayan battlefronts hardly a week after the Kota Bharu landing accelerated the big push south. Even if the Buffaloes (apt name), whose maximum speed was a hundred miles per hour, were still around, they would have been no match for the 175mph-plus Zero or Zeke. Britain might have had good reason for retaining for 'home defence' the more manoeuvrable and faster fighters, but it is worth putting on record that the Buffalo was obsolete in 1941, and this was 1942. Britain started off with 120 Buffaloes on the peninsula, and whatever of these that survived were withdrawn to Java by the middle of December.

Soon after the battles at Kota Bharu (December 8) and at Jitra (December 12) in both of which British forces sustained very heavy casualties, rumour took the field on behalf of the Japanese. Truth and fiction were so inextricably mingled that nobody in all Malaya or Singapore knew which was which. There was, however, some truth in a story that emanated from Malay *kampongs* (villages) concerning the masquerade of Japanese soldiers as Malays. Armed with a smattering of the Malay language – '*tabay*' thanks, '*ayer*' water and '*makan*' food – they were said to have fanned out into village Malaya. In sarong, they differed little from the Malays. The average Malay being a good mixer, the Japanese soldier had little difficulty in lingering in a village until his mission was complete. But they faced one serious obstacle – the sound 'l'. While they were adept in the use of gutturals and nasals, the soft el would always trip them up. Malay becomes 'Marr ... ray'. This was their shibboleth.

At the Domei they asked me for the address of my father in India and I wrote it down. The Japanese gentleman looked hard at the village name, Mallapally. Had it not been for the circumstances, I would have laughed out loud when he pronounced it 'Marraparri'. But despite their nasal disability, the 'Information' contingent did marvellous work side by side with the fighting wing.

Unlike in Manchuria or China, General Yamashita's forces in Malaya were assisted by neither pack mules nor horses. Following research in Formosa early in 1940 and confirmed by field exercises in Japan, Formosa and Hainan island the following year, a brilliant Japanese tactician suggested the humble bicycle as a valued adjunct to the invasion army in place of the horse or mule used in the sub-zero temperature on Siberian borders. Because Japan had sold more than a million cheap bicycles to Malaya the previous decade, it was concluded that spares would not be problem in the difficult early stages. Another reason was that some of the finest paved roadways in the East were seen in Malaya and the roads are well protected on either side by rubber or natural forests. So the invasion army brought along a small contingent of bicycles for each division with bicycle repairers to each unit.

British generals – there were no less than five in Malaya at the time as against two with the invaders – dismissed the bicycle story as preposterous – until they saw aerial pictures of bicycle manoeuvres. After pushing the machines a mile or two on demolished roads and bridges – the retreating troops had ammunition to burn – the bicycle blitzkrieg would move on until the forward elements came in contact with the British. Then the bicycles would be dumped on the roadside with a soldier to guard, and the column would attack, plastering the defenders with machinegun fire.

The Japanese were known to be first-rate infiltrators, avoiding as far as possible a frontal attack. But in the 1941–42 campaign in Malaya they seemed to have discarded their aversion because of little success at Nomonhan, on the Siberian border, and in Central China. Instead they adopted, in general, the method of softening one sector of the opposing strongpoint with concentrated fire from artillery and infantry with an overall bombing by Zeroes, to be followed by an infantry raid – after, of course, a prayer to the *Tenno* and shouts of '*Banzai!*'

Rumour had seriously eroded British morale from the start. Strange notes in Malay, Hindi and English were widely airdropped at troop concentrations: 'Your arms dump, situated two metres from "X", is to be bombed at 2am tomorrow. If you want to see your Mamma PLEASE move out of the area before midnight.' Either the arms cache was moved south or the troops withdrawn, more often the latter. Such 'tactical withdrawals' followed in quick succession.

Despite assiduous denials in the English and vernacular press – Malay, Chinese and Tamil – the phantom stories spread. One had it that the Japanese, dressed in Malay sarongs, were resting in a Singapore hotel while fighting was going on in the north. To Westerners, Japanese in pants were indistinguishable from other Asians. They dreaded the approach of Asian servants at night. Is the nightcap poisoned? Is the house-boy really Chinese – or Japanese? Fear ruled the day – and night.

Singapore's famous, or infamous, night life caught on to a good thing. Harlots did a two-way business, one with their white clientele and the other, in information, reaching up to Saigon and

Tokyo. There were hundreds of these Mata Haris around.

Britain suffered heavy losses in the first week of the war, but I wouldn't attach much importance to the contention that the troops were not seasoned or were rushed into battle for the first time. This may or may not be true but the fact remains that one Japanese was fighting two British, mostly with ammunition seized from the latter. In human material, the Japanese were no better nor worse, but they were superior in everything else: tactics, strategy, weapons, fire power, and they were masters of innovation. They easily subdued Kuala Lumpur after the bitterly contested crossing of the Slim River as they did Ipoh after the Perak River crossing at Kuala Kangsar. After the retreating British had dynamited both the road and railway bridges over the Perak River, I was told, General Yamashita asked the commander of the railway troops how long it would take to repair the two bridges. The commander examined the damage and replied it would take roughly three weeks.

'One week,' snapped the *Tiger*.

The railway contingent worked day and night and finished the job in one week, and heavy vehicles, including tanks, began to clatter south again. What surprised the defending army even more was Yamashita's novel, unconventional techniques. In the first place, neither Percival nor his brain in London could seriously accept the possibility that an invader might land in the north and fight through the jungles and marshlands to Singapore, more than 500 miles south. It was only in the third week of January 1942 that Churchill realised that the alleged fortress of Singapore was not a fortress; great big guns facing the water on the south to protect the harbour but north of the island, that is, the landward front towards the Malayan peninsula was hardly defended at all, and bereft of any strongpoints.

Servicemen, if not the common man, might have heard a lot about a defence scheme, originally conceived by Maj.-Gen. W.G.S. Dobbie, GOC Malaya, in 1937 and put into practical shape by Air Chief Marshal Sir Robert Brooke-Popham, known under the code name of Matador. When the time was ripe – who can say when? – it was intended a British force would strike north from Malaya across the Thai frontier to occupy Singora and Patani, and a second force, called the Krahcol (may be for Krah Column) would advance into Thailand and occupy the position known as The Ledge – the best defensive point in the area. All this remained in the British imagination until it was too late. One regiment stationed in Penang was ordered to cross to the mainland and push north to occupy The Ledge. It moved as far as Alor Star and ran into the retreating British from Jitra. By the time they turned back the Rising Sun was fluttering from the Municipal Building in Georgetown in Penang. So this regiment, too, joined the trek to Singapore.

The British were further confounded by Japanese small-boat manoeuvres, first in Teluk Anson and then in Port Swettenham and Batu Pahat. Singapore remained in control of the Straits of Malacca and the airbase in Sumatra, thus blocking the east-west sea route. How then did the Japanese launches get to the Bay of Bengal? It was a sensation of the day in the newspapers, and more so at Fort Canning. An English translation of Colonel Tsuji's book, *Singapore: The Japanese Version*,[1] sheds revealing light on the mystery:

'The small boats to be used were roughly forty large and small motor boats used in the Singora landing which ... had been taken overland by road and rail to the Alor Star River. After being launched again there they were collected in the neighbourhood of Lumut at the mouth of the Perak River, together with about twenty other boats which had been captured at Penang. Altogether these boats carried a battalion of infantry – more or less – and they travelled along the coast in the rear of the enemy, ceaselessly menacing their retreat. The 1st Manoeuvres Unit, composed of the main strength of the 11th Regiment under the command of Colonel Watanabe, one section of mountain guns, and a section of Engineers, was selected to be ferried from point to point along the coast as required to harass the enemy's retreat.'

Churchill indignantly protested to General Wavell and rebuked General Percival, but nothing could stem the Japanese tide. They *banzai*-ed to almost with a stone's throw of Singapore by the last day of January 1942. Fifteen days later Singapore capitulated and over 120,000 poured into prisoner-of-war camps.

---

1 Published by Ure Smith, Sydney.

4

The Last Ditch

ONCE AGAIN the unexpected had happened. As daylight broke on January 31 about 30,000 British troops withdrew from Johore across the highly vulnerable Causeway, a land bridge, into the cul-de-sac of Singapore. Strange, but this operation was carried out without any Japanese interference. Apparently their planes were busy bottling up the entire Dutch East Indies to prevent another Dunkirk. Few things can be said to the credit of General Wavell's Far East Command but this mass withdrawal of British troops from Johore right under the nose of the enemy was considered at the time to be a signal achievement.

The 8th Brigade of the 9th Indian Division which defended Kota Bharu on December 8 had few left in its ranks for the last-ditch stand in Singapore. The Argylls ran a close second in degree of decimation. The battalion, numbering 880 all ranks in December, returned to Singapore after the Slim River disaster a mere 90 strong. Army cooks and bottlewashers[1] at the Argylls's base camp rushed to fill the ranks, making in all 250 strong for

---

1 Men who performed a range of menial tasks.

the inner bridgehead covering the Johore withdrawal. As soon as the Argylls piped themselves across the Causeway with *Hielan' Laddie*, the order went out for the immediate demolition of the Causeway and the sea flowed through a 70-foot gap. Malaya was thus written off, and Singapore itself was to be in hardly a fortnight.

Like Percival in his Battle Box in Fort Canning, most of us in Singapore city were on a grandstand scanning the sky for Zeroes. As we heard the explosions to the north we speculated on the nature of the new disaster, but later Chinese 'underground' sources confirmed that the Causeway had been breached. Officialdom confirmed 48 hours later that Singapore had no land contact with the peninsula. We were neatly bottled up.

Parenthetically, I may say how I or rather we, including Jose, had been driven to the comparative safety of the city in preference to a risky sea voyage back to India. Mr Glover, at whose instance I came over to Singapore in 1938 as leader-writer, took a paternal interest in my affairs. For in those days neither in London nor in the colonial territories like Singapore was it considered healthy to have Asians as leader-writers. In the prewar era an Asian, if highly educated abroad, preferably at Oxford or Cambridge, might turn out to be a good subeditor but as leader-writer he would be like the devil in the world of angels. I would have been a journalistic also-ran but for Mr Glover's unobtrusive condescension. My presence on the *Tribune* made it somehow questionable in the eyes of the British, but our circulation, mostly among Asians, almost doubled within less than two years of my arrival. Advertising revenue soared, as did Mr Glover's reputation for making money.

In the beginning my employers, too, seemed to be badly shaken by my mild coffee colour. On seeing my first letter, they thought 'P Joseph John' might at least be an Anglo-Indian. But I am not one of that class. Most of my European and Eurasian colleagues were unsure of my longevity on the editorial desk, but Mr Glover and Mr (later Dato, a Malayan honour) SQ Wong, a Chinese director of the paper, early discovered whatever talents I had. The former allocated to me a sparsely furnished office with a few tomes on Malaya, and on the day after my arrival in the country (October 1938) asked me to write two leading articles on Malaya's Budget. Although I was green to Malaya's economy and politics (there was little at the time of the latter apart from tall talk, mostly post-prandial, by colonial officials), I wrote a thousand words on the Budget and sent up the typed sheets to Mr Glover for his okay. I must confess I was a little nervous. After reading the article, the editor-in-chief quickly consulted his senior associates and rushed into my room to congratulate me. The leader was sent down to be type-set for the day's paper and I had thus 'arrived' in the Malaya–Singapore newspaper world. So did Japanese forces at the southern extremity of the Malay Peninsula, three years later, on January 31, 1942.

Thinking it was his prime duty to see me out of the country before the Japanese entered the city, Mr Glover relieved me of my editorial responsibilities on January 15, four days after the Japanese occupation of Kuala Lumpur. With a fat cheque in my pocket I fled to my newly rented flat in Middle Road to brood over the changed circumstances with Jose. We had heard stories of various craft, bound for India or Australia, being either sunk or impounded by the Japanese Navy off the outer roads of Singapore harbour. We decided to stay put – and see the last moments of that 'Gibraltar of the East.'[2] Neither would ever regret that decision which gave us the opportunity to witness yet another facet of this earthly existence.

Civilian morale was low, with new rumours each day. A notorious story that went the round warned people not to use their closets because the Japanese had planted a soldier with a small ammunition dump in every closet in Singapore city. It found credence and I still wonder why. Public urinals and lavatories were shunned like the plague. Women were petrified; 'X' saw what looked like a Japanese soldier fleeing before her bedroom window in the middle of the night, and on seeing 'Y' another fled from her backyard.

Rumours of this type played such havoc that people began to doubt the British Army's 'mopping-up' operations. The common man in Singapore knew his time was up, whatever the British Army might or might not do. If there is to be another war in Asia, I would say that the army command might get fuller support from the civilian population if they could devise some mode of expression other than 'mopping-up' to indicate withdrawal.

In the city, law and order relapsed into momentary anarchy. Chinese, Malays or Indians in their tens of thousands looted

---

2 Bristling with big guns, facing south to the sea, the wrong way.

every unguarded shop, home or godown. But soon the army put a stop to this popular mania. Then there was the underworld, busy exchanging comestibles, liquor, cigarettes, cosmetics down to French aids and birth control, etc., for gold.

Fort Canning's Battle Box became busier. Now that the enemy was within sight, Percival seemed to have given the *quietus* to mopping-up. Instead, he called on civilians to 'dig or die for victory', conserve the water supply, etc. After the Japanese twin thrust at the island a week hence, the GOC's bland, censor-inspired prose didn't speak of mopping-up but asserted bravely: 'Elsewhere on the island there is no change in the situation. It is hoped to stabilise our position ... Continuous enemy pressure ... slackened during the night.' Good, a positive approach to truth. Nothing else would do at the time because the sands of Singapore's history were fast dripping away to a three-and-a-half-year interregnum.

Though everyone knew that the city's end was near, the rush on the harbour had eased, probably because of the Japanese Navy. The greater part of the civilian population was Chinese, Overseas Chinese, most of whom had little connection with mainland China. Malaya was their home from home. But most of the Chinese detectives who worked on the 'Japanese Wing' of the CID were given facilities to leave for Australia or India 'for the duration'. However, I knew several of them who decided to remain on the island and see it through. Newspapermen were given the same option. Some, whose names appeared over anti-Japanese articles, fled, while others like me remained.

It was soon known in the city that the naval base was being

dynamited, days before the expected Japanese invasion of the island. Morale couldn't have been lower than the floating dock which was sent to the bottom of the Johore Strait.

Much as I abhorred it, I had occasion in Singapore, before and after the surrender, to see racial animosities coming to a head – and erupting. I used the expression racial animosities not only to refer to the East as against the West but also to other inter-racial minorities, particularly Asian, seen in Singapore. The Japanese were soon exhibiting their sword skills on those Chinese they chose to label 'Communist cut-throats.' As for Indians, they had to thank Bose's escape to Germany from his closely guarded home in Calcutta early in 1941. The part he was to play later was then a secret in the Nazi Foreign Office, shared, by then, perhaps with Tokyo. It was rather strange that the Japanese were fawning on Indians, almost mollycoddling them, from the day they set foot in Singapore.

On February 2 began the continuous bombing not only of military installations but the city as a whole. On that day the siren wailed, not to stop until the 15th when Singapore surrendered. It was said there were a few Buffaloes or Hurricanes on Kallang airfield but none could be seen from our grandstand in Middle Road. Japanese planes by the hundreds came non-stop over the city bombing shipyards, shops, oil dumps, offices, barracks and Chinatown. With so much death and destruction around, few bothered about taking shelter while the siren screamed non-stop. There were still some people about dodging bombs or bullets to reach some ship or sampan leaving the blazing city. Never can I forget our enchanted haven in Middle Road. There was a ring of fire around the building, flames leaping hundreds of feet. Nothing remained of a fashionable department store in our street but burning embers after a flight of Japanese planes went past. Jose and I sneaked out when there was a pause in the bombing. The first thing we saw was a giant khaki-clad *jaga* (watchman) in the middle of the road. He was dead; the smile on his face still haunts me. Limbs of every description – European, Indian, Chinese, Malay and Eurasian – were everywhere.

The curtain rose at midnight, February 7, on the tragicomedy of Singapore under Japanese occupation.

5

Final Blunder

SINCE THEIR withdrawal from Johore Bharu on the morning of January 31 a story gained currency, by accident or design, that the British troops were withdrawing into Singapore to use the island as a Trojan horse. Throughout the pre-invasion week it was widely held in Singapore streets (certainly not in Fort Canning) that the British had some trick up their sleeves. They would let the Japanese 'snake' lie low but would annihilate it in one fell blow as soon as its hood was up. Or the British were just waiting for the whole of Japanese armour to advance deep into the peninsula before the Royal Navy would land troops somewhere off Penang and smash the invader in a murderous vice. Ah, such stories were a fine shower upon our parched lips, and repetition sweetened them. That this was a mere figment of hyper-active imagination was borne out by the events of February 8.

The previous night's landing on Pulau Ubin, a rocky islet in the narrow strip of water between the peninsula and Singapore, by the Japanese Imperial Guards was quickly followed by the withdrawal from that islet of a British unit posted there. From here the Japanese were hardly within a stone's throw of the huge naval base at Seletar, completed months before my arrival in the country in 1938. An instance of faulty intelligence was that, with the occupation of Pulau Ubin, Fort Canning jumped to the conclusion that the final all-out attack would come from that sector, the north-east, and so re-arranged the front-line to concentrate the best troops there. This was exactly what Yamashita anticipated. It was generally known in Japan that the Imperial Guards were not, as far as possible, used as front-line troops and that they were generally held as second-line forces. This was a noose which Yamashita dangled before Percival into which the head of the entire British forces on the island was thrown.

Though a lone Japanese is probably the least harmless in the world, two or more (with somebody to order them) are as invincible as any troops in the world of a like number. The British had not bothered to dissect the Japanese too minutely on the China front. The performance figures of the Japanese Zero, furnished by the British Ambassador in Chungking in 1940, were allowed to gather dust in Singapore archives. If these figures were analysed at the time Britain would not have sent those obsolete Buffaloes, Hurricanes or Wildebeests to protect her greatest showpiece in the Far East. By the time the envoy's figures were finally unearthed it was too late to catch up with the Zero[1]. The Spitfires were all reserved for the Battle of Britain.

The Imperial Guards, dress-up stars at the Imperial Court in Tokyo, were also brave fighting men but as a rule they were

---

1 In due course the Americans manufactured better and faster fighter aircraft.

condemned to the second string in battle. Yet, in the event, the main strength of the Imperial Guards crossed the straits a little to the west of the shattered Causeway despite heavy British artillery fire, and participated in the fighting on the island, reaching McRitchie Reservoir by the evening of Sunday, February 15. Another unit of the Guards pushed on to a point west of Kallang airport. As the Japanese saw it, the Imperial Guards had finally lived down much of the old criticism that they were soft.

The Guards' occupation of Pulau Ubin was a mere blind. It fooled Percival into concentrating his crack troops in the eastern sector, leaving the western sector thinly manned by the 22nd Australian Brigade. The Japanese reacted in true form. The 5th and 18th Divisions moved south from Scudai under an umbrella of rubber and crossed the straits behind the Imperial Guards about midnight on February 7. Big guns on either side of the straits, the British in the south and the Japanese in the north, lit up the coast. Mysteriously, the searchlights did not light up. After the lapse of decades no satisfactory explanation has yet come as to why they did not work at zero hour. I have heard it said later that the man with the keys of the searchlight unit was drunk and incapable somewhere in Singapore that fateful night. This may or may not be true, but I have also heard it stated that the unit was under instructions not to expose the lights to the heavy bombing which preceded the Japanese attack. This sounds equally puerile. Anyway, Verey lights had to be fired from GHQ to discover the fact that strings of Japanese motor launches were coming over. Whether due to British ineptitude or Japanese ingenuity, Japanese casualties in the battle for Singapore were a mere 5,092, dead and wounded. This might have been trebled or quadrupled if the searchlight unit had gone into operation. By the time the searchlights finally opened up, the invader had stolen into the mangrove swamps behind which the hapless Australians waited breathlessly. With the murderous drumfire of the initial bombardment ringing in their ears, the Australians fell back to a safer perimeter, a mile south. And that was the beginning of the steady unrolling of the carpet.

The Japanese may or may not still believe it was their valour that led to the British surrender in so short a time. I do admire their valour which was, and still is, no superior to anybody else's. There were instances of Japanese refusal to stand up to bombardment on the front-line. If they happened to get one, two or three successive blows the Japanese would wilt like anybody else. Nor do I desire to convey the impression that the British[2] were running away all the time. The ship blaze at Kota Bharu and the artillery frightened a section of the Japanese who tried to get away by ship not to Japanese-controlled Indo-China, but to China's Hainan island or Formosa[3]. In the final analysis, the invader was much more ingenious than the British who appeared, in Malaya at any rate, to be more ingenuous.

The early defeats in North Malaya had sapped British morale. Similar was the story in Singapore. The Tengah airfield

---

2 Empire troops included Indian, Australian and New Zealand elements.
3 Both occupied by Japan.

was occupied in the evening of the 9th, less than 24 hours after the first Japanese landing. By this time Yamashita had shifted his headquarters to the island. He well knew the British were not going to continue the struggle: why else had they abandoned the naval base days before his army had landed in Singapore?

The rest of the Singapore story is simple. After the seizure of the Tengah airfield and the Bukit Timah heights, the Japanese 5th Division was poised for a drive into the city by Bukit Timah Road on January 11, the day of Kigensetsu, an important national festival for the Japanese. Although the High Command in Tokyo had given them 100 days to capture and subdue Singapore, the Japanese fighting services in the field had so excelled themselves as to make some expect that the fortress would fall on Kigensetsu. Anyway, The Tiger chose to give the British four more days when, according to the Kempeitai (Military Information Department), a new city was to be born: Shonan, the Light of the South.

About the time the floating dock was sunk in the Johore Straits, the naval base underwent a sort of demolition simultaneous with the withdrawal of 'defence experts' to Padang, in Sumatra, or Colombo. Whether the demolition of the base was partial or complete, as events later proved, Singapore did not play any part in bringing peace to a war-weary world.

From the very beginning, the Japanese advance was replete with surprise. Their forces that drove from the west were specially equipped for night attack through marshland. They were said to have been broken into small units of 10 men, each led by a monitor with a luminous compass strapped to his wrist, and detailed maps of Singapore, so much so that at any given point of the compass or time the monitor could easily say where the nearest road lay. No wonder they easily turned the Australian flank. The defenders in this area were mostly green recruits. Those who did not fall in battle were either plodding about in marshland or rubber estates or were withdrawn in great hurry to a southern defence position. As daylight broke on the 9th many of the survivors found themselves deep in enemy country. The withdrawal had thoroughly demoralised them – as well as those who saw the ragged lot.

To put it blandly, the Australians did not have men with compasses strapped to their wrists, and for many of them the small stretches of jungle in the western sector – I cannot bring myself to call it the Western Front, a name which the British of a previous generation had made famous in France – were a terrifying maze even without enemy troops lurking in them. Groups of men became separated from their comrades in the bewildering darkness. Some straggled back as far as Bukit Timah. Others even reached Singapore city; the disorganisation was complete long before they could be picked up, reorganised and sent back. The 29th Australians was no longer a cohesive fighting force.

Before the week ended Japanese armour reached the outskirts of the city. Most of the Allied regiments – Australian, British, Indian, Malay, etc. – had retreated into the city or the suburbs. Since the rupture of the Causeway pipeline the city depended on its own meagre supply from McRitchie reservoir, and flat dwellers discovered that water was just a trickle even at street level. Food supplies, if preserved, might feed the city at least six months. The situation was indeed hopeless, and Percival might be excused for not destroying the city by house-to-house fighting as insisted by Churchill. Hours before he stood before The Tiger that fateful Sunday evening, the bulk of Allied troops had been massed at landmarks such as Fullerton Building, the Supreme Court, municipal buildings and the *padang*, for something to happen. Most had read, or heard of, the airdropped Japanese leaflets (enclosed in wooden boxes and addressed to the British GHQ) calling upon 'Your Excellency' to 'give up this meaningless and desperate resistance and promptly order the entire front to cease hostilities, and to dispatch at the same time your parliamentaire according to the procedure shown at the end of the advice.'[4]

On Friday the 13th some more Japanese boxes were airdropped. They contained the following admonition from the Nippon Army:

I have the honour of presenting to you this Admonition of Peace from the standpoint of the Nippon Samurai Spirit. Nippon Navy, Army and Air Force have conquered he Philippine Islands and Hong Kong and annihilated the British extreme Oriental Fleet in the Southern Seas. The command of the Pacific Ocean and the Indian Ocean as well as the Aviation power in the Southern and

---

4 The Parliamentaire, bearing a white flag and the Union Jack, should proceed to Bukit Timah Road.

Western Asian Continents is now under the control of Nippon Forces. India has risen in rebellion. Thai and Malaya have been subjected to the Nippon without any remarkable resistance. The war has almost been settled already and Malay is under Nippon Power. Since the 18th century, Singapore has been the starting point of the development of your country and the important juncture of the civilisation of the West and East. Our Army cannot suffer as well as you to see this district burn to ashes by the war. Traditionally when Nippon is at war, when she takes her arms, she is always based upon the loyalty and breaking wrong and helping right and she does not and never aims at the conquest of other nations nor the expansion of her territories.

The war cause, at this time, as you are well aware, originated from this loyalty. We want to establish new order and some of the mutual prosperity in the Eastern Orient. You cannot deny at the bottom of your impartial hearts that this is divine will and humanity to give happiness to millions of East Orientals mourning under the exploitation and persecution. Consequently the Nippon Army, based upon this great loyalty, attacks without reserve those resist them, but not only the innocent people but all the surrendered to them will be treated kindly according to their Samuraism. When I imagined the state of mind of you who have so well done your duty, isolated and without rescuer, and now surrounded by our Armies, how much more could I not sincerely sympathise with you. This is why I do advise you to make peace and give you a friendly hand to co-operate for the settlement of the Oriental Peace. Many thousands of wives and children of your

Officers and Soldiers are heartily waiting in their Native Land to the coming home of their husbands and fathers and many hundreds of thousand of innocent people are also passionately wishing to avoid the calamities of War.

I expect you to consider upon the eternal honour of British Tradition, and you, be persuade by this Admonition. Upon my word, we won't kill you, but treat you as Officers and Soldiers if you come to us. But if you resist us we will gibe swords.
Nippon Army
Singapore,
13 Feb. 42

It was Churchill's dogged perseverance that persuaded Wavell, and through him Percival, to prolong the fruitless war to the 15th of February. If he had his way, Percival would have surrendered a few days earlier because he knew he was well and truly beaten with no escape. From Thursday, three days before the surrender, Loyals, Manchesters and Argylls, not to mention Australians, could be seen packing into buildings on the southern seaboard. Reller's Band at the Adelphi or the swing band at the Raffles Hotel had night-long khaki-clad audiences. Practically every cinema in the city was full. The greatest attraction was the raunchy *Ziegfeld Follies*[5] with bumper houses at the Cathay. However, the artillery kept up an increasing barrage. They had munitions for six months, and they might as well.

---

5 Probably a knock-off of the popular Broadway musical.

After the early morning church service on Sunday, February 15, Percival called a conference of senior commanders and key civic officials and told them he had been granted permission to capitulate, if need be. His commanders were convinced that a counter-attack was out of the question, and Percival finally decided to give in.

6

The Sunrise

THERE WAS AN unearthly quiet in the whole of the island from the night of the surrender up to 48 hours or more. Even the cicada, whose orchestral concert is almost an integral part of nightlife in the Far East, appeared to have gone on strike. Only selected groups from the Japanese rank and file were allowed to enter the shattered city, which was all rubble and ruin from Newton to Raffles Quay, from Pasir Panjang to Katong. With the thousands who lay buried under the debris in Chinatown, the total civilian casualties in Singapore was estimated to be between five thousand and six thousand, far outstripping military casualties in the island. And the horror was that most of the civilian dead could not be seen because they were buried under tonnes of debris. The pervading stench told its own story of the intense week-long bombardment.

It was a ghost city. With the disappearance of most of the landmarks, picking one's way through the smouldering streets became a laborious task. On the morning of Feb. 16, the first day under the new military regime, I walked the one and a half miles from my Middle Road flat to Raffles Place. It took almost two hours. I had to tiptoe through the debris to avoid live wires that criss-crossed the streets and partially blasted walls that swayed with the wind. It could all have ended there and then for me when I stepped on an insignificant strand of wire protruding from a razed block of flats. Luckily, I felt only a mild shock.

Most of the streets were ploughed by incessant bombing and machinegun fire. There were yawning chasms where some large building had simply vanished. Swarms of flies hovered over vegetating human waste all along the streets. Raffles Place, normally the hub of Malaya's economic life and Singapore's Covent Garden, was practically dead and hollow, enveloped by a cloud of flies. The old department store, Robinsons, was bombed the first week of the war, and it continued its charmed existence until war's end in a rented building in Malacca Street. Assisted by a flank of Indian boys on either side, I saw Chinese looters clearing out several shops and godowns. But most of the liquor had already gone down the drain. I was told some two hundred men spent a whole day breaking bottles so that the perpetually thirsty Japanese would not get a drop of it. The British took the cue from Hong Kong where the Japanese seized all the liquor stocks the day of the port's surrender at Christmas 1941, drank themselves silly, and plundered and raped. We were spared the bestiality, but every clink of a broken bottle may also have broken the hearts of the brewers and distillers. Some ten million Straits dollar notes were burned the previous day. The conquerors brought with them their own currency which at bayonet point was passed on a par with the old dollar. Unpegged (to yen) as they were, these Japanese notes in a year or two slumped to dirt. Barter came into play towards the end of Shonan; for a quarter-measure of Thai rice you would be lucky if you could procure M & B pills, which became priceless.

What struck me most that day was the eerie silence. Passers-by were few and far between, and they never spoke above a whisper. It was the very heart of Singapore, and it beat rather imperceptibly. Most of the people in Raffles Place melted away on seeing a small batch of Japanese technicians who came to repair the telephone lines. I was astonished to note how puny those fellows were. I wondered how they neatly smoked out the British from Singapore. Not with their muscles.

Japanese staff cars were seen plying the streets in regular succession. Because they were not kow-towed to by the city folk some of the officers became very annoyed. British soldiers as well as civilians were often asked to pay obeisance to the Nippon Army while moving on the roads as if nothing special had happened to the British Lion. Nippon knew she had, for a time, clipped the poor lion's tail. But from all that I saw that day the lion was apparently unaware of its disfigurement!

The full name of the sacred principle that was said to animate Japan's every action during the last war was the Greater East Asia Co-Prosperity Sphere. Unlike the *Toa Renmei Undo* (East Asia Federation Movement) organised in 1931 by Maj.-Gen. Kanji Ishihara, the Japanese thought the Co-Prosperity Sphere of 1942 was milder or mellower in import. It was thought that the new concept would so catch up with the Asian masses as to prevent any further bloodshed. The rank and file of the Japanese Army turned to Tokyo and tearfully prayed for their fallen comrades and paid obeisance to *Tenno-Heika* whenever opportunity presented itself. But for the present the fruits of victory were entirely theirs. The common man, or rather the common soldier, fell far short of the high, oh very high, ideals the Nippon High Command pumped into the soldier abroad. Army discipline is extremely stringent in Nippon, and while in Shonan I had heard of exemplary punishment being meted out to commanders for rape, looting or shoplifting. Some who were so punished in Malaya had to be kept under round-the-clock surveillance to see that they did not commit *hara-kiri* (suicide by disembowelling). Even today it terrifies me to contemplate what would have happened to the hapless civilian population if the Japanese had to fight through the overfilled streets of Singapore right up to the waterfront.

The common man you met in the Ginza in Tokyo yesterday, the one you meet today, and will meet tomorrow, typifies all that you have heard of the extreme courtesy of the Japanese. I have had the rare privilege of being associated with educated Japanese of the day, and it was really difficult to believe that both the violent private who ran amok on seeing the edge of a skirt and the delicate Buddhas of Nippon society came from the same stock. I would like to believe what a senior army officer once told me: 'War excites passions; peace restores tranquillity'. What he meant was this: 'When khaki is discarded at home we are all Buddhas'. From all that I know of present-day Japan she seems to be once again isolating herself from the outside bellicose world, concentrating upon the making of all manner of things from pins to tape-recorders, transistors, 'fun on two wheels', etc. It is the ardent hope of everybody that long may she continue doing something for peace, and Asia's prosperity and economic wellbeing.

Europeans, soldiers as well as civilians, and quite a few Eurasians were immediately bundled off to the Changi detention camp. With them went a section of Indian soldiers who stuck to army discipline while nearly 90 per cent of them, out of patriotism or personal convenience, affirmed their loyalty to India and also to Nippon to the extent she helped India in wresting her freedom from the British Raj. Though it was then known in the Nippon high command that Subhas Babu (who later came to be known as Netaji) was waiting in Berlin, Shonan was totally in the dark as to his whereabouts. On Bose's first appearance in Shonan the following year almost all the Indian prisoners of war streamed to the Padang where he first made his public speech calling for blood, sweat and tears to wrest the freedom of his country that had been bled white by British imperialists. India's war cry '*Challo Dilli!*'[1] reverberated all over the island. And many Indians, men as well as women, who had never seen a rifle in all their lives, rushed to the colours. India's were, and are today, green, white and saffron.

The Nippon flag was much in evidence that day. Almost every Indian soldier I saw in the streets that day had buttonholed the Rising Sun and it proved a veritable talisman against molestation from Japanese troops. '*Indo-jin, ka?*' queried a Japanese officer,

---

1 Go to Delhi.

and the Indian party exclaimed '*Challo Dilli!*' I almost hummed as I retraced my steps back to Middle Road where Jose and I had to plan out our new life most carefully and share the household chores. Our task had been considerably lightened by the unexpected return home of Krishna, our cook, who tried to get away in some ship at least a dozen times in the last fortnight. Like me he, too, was a Malayalee. And in the three and a half years of the Japanese occupation he showed us some clever culinary somersaults by which a grain of rice was made to do the job of ten.

I pondered my own problem. Hardly three weeks had gone by since I stopped writing venomous anti-Japanese editorials for the *Tribune*. Was I not a fit candidate for the Japanese to shoot as soon as I was discovered? No, the Japanese wouldn't shoot one if he or she can be disembowelled. Cartridges are too costly to be expended on unarmed creatures.

Days rolled by. At home we had a veritable grocery store with enough coffee, tea, sugar, rice, wheat and other provisions to last us at least two years. We had also stored some liquor, just where the bottles were secreted only Krishna knew.

Jose insisted that I should remain at home in future, as far as possible in our bedroom. After breakfast everyday he was to go to the terrace to scan the neighbourhood without exposing himself too much. Again after luncheon and a nap, he would resume his vigil until sunset. For a few weeks before the surrender Jose had worked as a clerk in the War Department and was highly nervous whenever Japanese cars passed our door, not only for his own safety but for mine, too. And Krishna soared to new heights in the culinary arts. His *mee,* a Chinese dish of fried vermicelli garnished with greens and chicken or fish, was simply marvellous. As time wore on, neither chicken nor greens could be obtained in the market, and still Krishna managed to keep us on our feet.

The more we thought of escape the greater the confusion became. Friends called by to see if all was well, and I gathered that the Kempeitai was searching the city for ex-newspapermen, and that Indians were generally treated with compassion. But those who knew what position I held on the *Tribune* had fears for my personal safety. February came to an end.

Before the British prisoners were removed from Changi to Burma, Korea or Formosa they were detailed to clean the streets. Most of them had shoes or boots in the initial stages but in time many were unshod, The prisoners' own workshop in camp produced contraptions made of wood, worn-out leather or anything handy for the soles. The Japanese wanted Asians to see their ex-bosses sweeping the streets and cleaning drains every morning, although few among the educated classes lingered to see this sign of providential topsyturvydom. Japanese photographs of this operation showed large crowds of Chinese interspersed thinly with Indians looking on as Westerners swept the streets or cleaned the drains. It did give them food for thought, but it did not make them look down on the poor souls reduced to such menial tasks, nor did the operation persuade us to look upon the Japanese as saviours. As I look back the main thought that remains in my mind is that the Japanese should have left behind in the Asian mind a far better picture of the true spirit of Nippon than what they actually did.

The Chinese appeared to be far more resourceful and calculating than the Japanese. Despite the various forms of cruelty to which they were subjected, the Overseas Chinese of Malaya came out of it all quite creditably. Most of their businessmen's money was in safe-keeping in London or New York throughout the war years. Besides the total extermination of *Dallforce*[2] the Overseas Chinese community in Malaya lost a few thousand of its members after the British surrender. They slogged through utter destitution and privation to emerge as vital as ever. Swords were aimed at their necks as millions of dollars were raised from them as a donation to Japan's war effort.

As I write this I hear that China is putting great store by her first atomic detonation in 1964, with more nuclear tests to follow. Will China blunder into a Pearl Harbour of some sort? The noises coming out of Beijing give me a sense of deja vu. Few in the world at that time expected Japan's sensational downfall in 1945. Her steamroller advance through Malaya and the swift capture of the fortress of Singapore had given Japan almost complete control of the western Pacific. Had it not been for the first atom bomb, made by the so-called Manhattan District Engineers in the United States, Japan would have held out a few more years causing

---

2 A hastily cobbled together force made up mostly of young Chinese volunteers and a few British survivors from the Malayan campaign.

greater destruction and loss of life, in Japan as well as the rest of Asia and world.

7

The Tedium

EACH DAY IN new Shonan appeared to be exactly like the previous – if you hadn't been nabbed by the military police or had not dropped dead in the street due to sheer hunger. The Chinese are perhaps more meticulous than Indians or Malays in not letting a soul hear of starvation they might be condemned to. So long as my temporary home in Middle Road was not detected by the Japanese as one occupied by a man urgently needed by the secret police, all seemed quiet and undisturbed. After a few days of extreme nervousness during which Jose and I violently shivered in our pants (or sarongs) every time we caught sight of a passing jeep or truck, we gradually appeared to regain our composure and stuck to our routine previously agreed upon – I would be closeted in the bedroom, and he would keep watch from the terrace. Ah, the exquisite joy of doing nothing!

There were about fifty of my countrymen within easy reach. Often they called at our home to see if all was well. Invariably, the conversation between friends, or even strangers in Shonan, began something like this: 'Have you eaten?' The implication was that the inquirer had in his possession a measure of rice to spare if the reply was in the negative. In the early stage of the occupation, the reply (murmured) was: 'Yes, had light gruel. Tapioca is a godsend.'

That Japanese soldiers were in your latrine or outhouse with arms dumps was a persistent rumour that sapped the morale of Singapore society a few weeks before the surrender. In Shonan, too, this rumour was revived with telling effect, I do not know by whom. Like every one of its ilk, this rumour too flew at more than lightning's speed all over the residential areas of the city so much so that not a word was even whispered in any home. All quiet on the home front. The rarest commodity in Shonan, next to rice, was speech. Though most opportune, the ruling silence was indeed eerie, especially at night.

By long association on the battlefield, most Japanese could decipher Mandarin, contrary to appearances. We from Kerala (the south-western State of India), on the other hand, are most fortunate. Very few, I might even say none, outside the community, speak or understand Malayalam. We chattered away without any outsider getting wise. Usually, we yarned away with friends in our drawing room until about six in the evening when everybody dispersed. After 7pm no one could be seen on the streets except soldiers on duty. Weren't we law abiding? When it was decreed that water was strictly to be rationed if the present supply was to last until the repairs were completed, I knew many who trekked to kampongs miles away, to draw water from village wells and carried it all the way back to the city.

Shonan, so long as it lasted, was the most gentle and law-abiding city ever seen on the face of the earth. Apparently, the large Chinese population did not really subscribe to the old Chinese belief that foreign gunpowder was powerless against true sons of China. They also knew that Japanese swords were as sharp as their own and could sever heads just as easily. Had they not seen Chinese heads rolling in the dust of Shonan as well as in Malaya? So, all appeared quiet in Malaya and Singapore except civilian stomachs which growled when there was no money to pay for rice.

Naturally, every able-bodied man and woman rushed to wherever jobs could be had, and the employers, to begin with, were exclusively Japanese. Priority was given to repair of harbour installations, aerodromes, railways and roads. And everybody, man or woman, had to be rigorously screened before being re-employed. Ex-employees were given preference but the screening was done with the aid of old police officers who themselves were screened or purged before being re-engaged. For one reason or another the police cast away a large proportion of the applicants, and from these castaways some were picked up for eventual liquidation. Others went underground to linger on as best they could, or until The Reaper's sickle shortened their misery. Many went north into the jungle to form the nucleus of Communist guerrillas who proved such a headache to the Japanese. Even after Japanese capitulation they fell foul of the British who found it difficult to concede the Reds' demands for reparation. And Sir Gerald Templer, the post-war High Commissioner of Malaya, had to fight them for nearly eight years before they were finally beaten.

Before they sailed from Indo-China, the Japanese forces were not only armed to the teeth but were also given a secret dossier on newspapermen. My name was among the first twelve qualified by the remark, 'author of several anti-Nippon articles'. From early December the Kempeitai had been scouring town after town behind their fighting forces to capture the named 'criminals'. As they arrived in Singapore in February the search for missing links was intensified. I was almost written off the list as 'untraceable; apparently left the country'. But Malayan detectives were combing the streets daily and eventually information reached them that I hadn't left the country and so ought to be 'somewhere in or around Singapore'.

Condemned to house arrest, as it were, reading became boring. By the middle of March, London charivari in the form of *Punch* or *The Times'* weekly supplement of which I had two years' copies on my files fast began to lose my interest. And I began to move out further from home – until I was spotted by police informers. They tried to size me up by putting to me some questions on the weather (which, said I, was infinitely more glorious than I had ever experienced), ranging gradually down to questions about the 'new times'. To the last query I warmly responded: 'Most stirring times indeed! I can almost hear bricks being laid, one by one, to build Asia for Asians.' A bit highfaluting for the occasion, I'd say. They didn't even ask me where I was living (of course, they were shadowing me).

The following morning the Kempeitai had a fairly full report of my conversation with their agents or informers. Why they pigeon-holed my dossier for more than five weeks I couldn't fathom. Maybe there was some advice from Tokyo, whatever the reason, I got some more days of peace and tranquillity, and I reverted to *Punch*. We would also play auction bridge that kept us busy all of daylight hours. Although the blackout had been lifted, most people remained indoors, with lights dimmed. What this meant in a city whose population is predominantly Chinese most of whom dine out in coffee stalls or pavements, only those acquainted with Singapore's nightlife could appreciate. Even rich *towkays*, with their harems and hangers-on, and old women ignoring their painful bound feet, usually went out for dinner for anything from a bowl of rice gruel to shark's fin soup and fried rice. Missing was the ubiquitous click-clack of Chinese clogs.

At the time, there were three amusement halls or parks in Shonan and they were allowed to reopen after the Chinese owners had been purged. The new proprietors extended the purge to all employees, down to boys at the gate and *amahs*, all starch and discipline, looking after the *tuan besar's* myriad offspring. The 'amusements' were amended to conform to the fiats issued from time to time. All foreign liquor that remained was removed case by case to the Japanese Army's GHQ in the former Fort Canning, leaving locally brewed *samsu* for general indulgence. Some bar owners were hauled off to jail because their *samsu* tasted like foreign liquor! One gentleman explained that it tasted so good because of many years of maturing.

In spite of court orders and Japanese army 'admonitions', the wealthy gave themselves hearty meals every day while 'The Canker' remained with them. The euphemism for the Japanese

Occupation lasted right up till the end. Even so, there were millions of people, not only in Singapore but all over Malaya and large parts of Asia, who couldn't find the wherewithal for even a cup of *kopi-o* (black coffee) every day. There was acute distress – until the Japanese reopened rubber estates and tin mines. Those who couldn't find a job with the new masters had either to languish until they were captured by the Kempeitai on suspicion of underground activities, or jump the gun and flee into the jungle and join the Communist guerrillas.

As months went by, Japanese technicians repaired the war damage and communications were restored. The Causeway was reopened after the 70-yard breach was closed, and trains ran to schedule from Singapore to Bangkok. All appeared to be normal, then began the crackdown on Communists, or those the Japanese chose to label so. Severed heads were displayed in Kuala Lumpur to persuade fence-sitters. In Singapore the work at the YMCA building, now occupied by military police, attracted wide publicity. Row after row of so-called suspects went in through one gate of our own Buchenwald and through another emerged as walking skeletons or lorryloads of corpses, mostly by night. There was the stillness of the cemetery throughout the city.

Eyes became hollow, whatever the pigmentation, from going days without food. As we entered April it was common to see women with bunches of babies and small children looking for a morsel of food. We gave away our supplies until a year's stock was down to a few months. Growing distress gave us courage of sorts to be charitable and not to give a thought for the morrow if the kitchen fire burned for the day. Sufficient unto the day was the evil thereof. We plodded on toward Canaan, the land of promise, which beckoned us from beyond the haze that shrouded us. But even the little food in our stock became a burden on the conscience when people started collapsing in the street due to sheer hunger. From my experience in occupied Singapore, I can say that differences of caste, colour or creed would crumble in the face of acute hardship. It was precisely so in Shonan. Himself tottering from hunger (it doesn't matter what his hue is) a breadwinner walked the city till sundown without encountering anybody who might give him a job, *any* job, or even a good Samaritan who might help him feed his emaciated wife and six children. He did not return home that day. And nobody knew what had happened to him. A fortnight later the woman found a letter secreted under her bed; it was only then that she discovered that she had been a fortnight-old widow. I know she and her six children survived the war because she learned Nippon-go and landed a job at the harbour.

History is written by survivors. It is the survivors of Shonan and their descendants who are building the new Singapore.

It was false prestige of the British, not lack of arms, that led to the virtual decimation of those gallant sons – and daughters, too – of Malaya, known as Dallforce, whose blood spilt in Singapore early in 1942 lends colour to the island's cannas and orchids today. The British had arms to burn. The advancing Japanese captured enough to fight for years without any imports from their fatherland. Unfortunately, the island's then overlords had little imagination. If they thought they themselves were strong enough to resist any attempt to invade the island, was it not cruel and unconscionable on their part to call on the poorly-armed Dallforce[1] to cover the British regiments' flanks?

In the sense that the War Office was not responsible for Dallforce, Britain probably could have avoided censure if a Royal Commission had gone into the British defeat in Singapore. Anyhow such a Commission was never appointed, the apparent aim being the need to avoid displaying dirty linen in the full blaze of publicity. The bulk of Dallforce were Chinese, Kuomintang and Communist, with a few Indians and Eurasians. Whether the young Chinese still believed the old saying that foreign gunpowder was useless against true sons and daughters of China, none could say. But chanting a breezy refrain that they were building a new Great Wall with their flesh and blood, Dallforce moved to guard the flanks of the British Army in the north-east of Singapore island and were wiped out *en masse*. Their weapons, or more aptly missiles ranging from crowbars and knuckledusters to sporting rifles, did little but attract machine-gun bullets. On nights when the moon is full and all is quiet I can sometimes hear that old Chinese tune like a whisper all the way from Singapore's fragrant forests.

---

[1] A Colonel Dalley set up the mixed unit of regulars and volunteers by the mouth of the Kranji River. He saw them before the assault and gave them orders not to retreat. The next morning he went back to look for Dallforce and discovered that one British officer and five other ranks had retreated safely. There were no wounded to bring back. Other members of the force had fought and died to the last man and woman.

Jose and I went on waiting, wondering what fearful visitations the morrow might bring – until the eve of my 36th birthday, April 21, 1942, the first year of Shonan.

8

Magic Lamp (1942)

IT WAS KRISHNA'S very last trick, or so it appeared. He wangled out of next-to-nothing a so-called dinner for twenty on my birthday. It was ersatz affair concocted out of two fowls, three measures of rice, an eight-ounce tin each of turnips and tomatoes, with liberal helpings of tapioca. The meal left a lot to be desired but nice words capped Krishna's inimitable culinary feat. No sooner had the sun gone down in the Indian Ocean in a crazily hued firmament to match the turmoil she was leaving behind than our guests – Buddhists, Christians, Hindus and Muslims – began to disperse after wishing us long life and prosperity galore, in spite of the fact we were fast sinking into stark poverty. The cupboard was almost empty. After a fitful sleep I rose rather early to greet my birthday. Boiled tapioca with chilli sauce and a cup of weak tea was now our breakfast. And soon Jose climbed to his terrace post.

About ten he hastened down and blabbered out something, motioning to a window. Tip-toeing to a corner of the window I saw a highly camouflaged Jeep that had pulled up on the kerb opposite the stairway to our flat. A soldier appeared and whispered something to the sphinxes in the vehicle, apparently providing them my floor and flat number. As the party stepped out of the Jeep, I entreated my brother to return to the terrace and lie prone on the cement floor. He hesitated and I had to use force (warily, in absolute silence) to make him leave me alone. I whispered to him that at least one of us ought to try and survive to tell the folks back home what happened. For a frightful minute we were locked in what appeared to be our final embrace. Jose disappeared and I was in the drawing room with the day's *Azad Hind*, an Indian-run paper under Japanese auspices, before me when an earthquake shook the door off its hinges. Two Japanese officers, armed to the teeth, covered the door with drawn revolvers. By instinct I got up with raised arms. The glare of their narrowed slant-eyes never wavered. The revolvers were pointed at my heart. Seconds ticked by. Then one of them hissed at me, '*In-greesu-ka? Indo-jin-ka?*' I surmised that the first stood for English and the second Indian. I blurted out 'Indo. . .' but the magic word failed to ease the tension. The two revolvers continued to terrorise me.

I cannot say how long the confrontation lasted but my wall clock chimed eleven and brought us all back to reality. Now a third Japanese who had hitherto remained in the background whispered something in the ears of the armed pair and pushed to the front. As if carefully memorised, he harangued me in Nippon-go to my utter consternation. I knew I had to say something but what? Almost every sentence he uttered ended in '*ka?*' The nearest English translation is 'isn't that so?' With the little smattering of Malay I knew and plenty of gestures I conveyed to them that maybe I should write my case-history in English, and after studying it they could do whatever they liked.

The pain in the sternum was become intense, for by then it was almost 45 minutes with my arms up in a sort of perpetual supplication. Mentally, I peeped into the kitchen where, following my long-term instructions, Krishna would have adjourned his culinary operations and sat cross-legged on the floor in otherworldly meditation. On the terrace my brother was getting roasted on the cement in the midday heat.

Ours was one among 39 flats divided into 13 on each floor, the total strength being roughly 300. Our world was composed mostly of Chinese with a few Eurasians, Indians, Malays, Jews and Arabs. It was almost like a miniature Singapore, with Europeans scored out. What camaraderie among us! One for all and all for one. The adults went door to door every day enquiring if they had *makan* (food). If the answer was no, out of nothingness emerged, hey presto!, a meal for the day. It was indeed miraculous how the population found its daily bread despite very heavy odds. I knew a Chinese gentleman who pawned his wife's bracelet with a rich *towkay* and raised a few thousand military dollars to pay for a couple of days' stock of rice. A week later the *towkay* was taken to the Japanese GHQ for questioning. Whether he ever returned home I do not know but the other chap, burdened with wife and seven children, was about to flounder when he landed a railway job. That family survived the war. But at the moment none could say if Jose and I would survive April 21.

I noticed a sly smile or sneer in a corner of my interrogator's hollow cheeks. He suddenly cast his mask aside and asked me in Standard Two English:

'Where your transmidder is? No transmidder, no life. Do not lie to us Nippon-jin.'

I replied in the best broken English I knew that I had never touched a transmitter in all my life, nor did I possess one. They started a search and I followed at a safe distance. It lasted about fifteen minutes. They snarled things when they saw some of the cartoons in the English magazines on the table, but a smile (or was it a grin) began to unloosen their severe features as they threw open the door of the kitchen-cum-store. It took some time for Krishna to arise from his prayerful abyss. He stretched out and then bowed in a delicate *namaskar*. My uninvited guests were not interested in Krishna or his flamboyant *namaskar* but motioned for meat-safe keys.

They opened the drawers one by one and made a note of everything. There was no liquor, thanks to Krishna. Each Japanese trousered a bottle of strawberry jam and we all returned to the drawing room to continue the interrogation. I was still holding my arms up. As we filed into the room I noticed a fourth Japanese on guard duty by the front door. From the kitchen door I also observed a few strange characters perched on stools at coffee stalls in the back alley. They were would-be detectives, more dangerous to civilian life than full-fledged detectives. They would do anything, lie about anyone, to worm into the graces of the conquerors. It struck me somewhat odd that there was absolute silence in our neighbourhood. The whole island had gone quiet in the days surrounding the British surrender but things had been looking up lately. Although few heads could be seen in the streets there was a gentle hum in the daytime in our part of the city which was thickly populated. Today there was complete silence. All had gone to sleep, it seemed, with or without food. The full strength of Singapore's detective force was no doubt in Middle Road that day.

My arms were now almost slipping from their joints. I well knew that the Japanese Army's panacea for all ills was quick seizure and instant destruction. Why then were they dilly-dallying with my life? The conversation went something like this:

Q: Transmidder no. agreed presently. If found after examination you will be pulverised. (Eh?) Did you not work for an anti-Nippon newspaper?

A: I worked for a pro-Asian, not anti-Japanese paper.

Q: What do you mean by pro-Asian? Pro-Asian is pro-Japanese, yes?

A: We ardently loved Asia, not to mention any country by name.

Q: What did you actually do for your paper every day?

A: I subedited cables, Reuter as well as Associated Press.

Q: Did you write leading articles?

A: Yes, on Indian affairs, once weekly.

At this stage I was mercifully asked to bring down my tottering arms.

After thanking my malevolent questioner for this welcome riddance, I faced them with a little more confidence. The cross-examination resumed.

Q: Have you heard of Subassu Boshji?

A: Yes, the sheet-anchor of Indian nationalism today. He escaped from Calcutta last year from the British who kept him under surveillance.

Q: Boshji[1] may be here in a few months. Will you march with him to India via Burma?

A: Of course I will, God permitting.

They appeared relieved. They flung their revolvers on the drawing room table and beckoned me to sit down. I did so, but bobbed up immediately to invite my untimely visitors to lunch. It was three already. I asked permission to go to the kitchen and ask Krishna to cook something. Reply being in the affirmative, I fled to the kitchen and asked Krishna, for God's sake, to produce a meal for four out of the blue. He dipped into his secret store and promptly produced, first a bottle of scotch and three bottles of Australian beer. I wondered whether the time was opportune to confess that I had a brother on the terrace being baked crisp. I decided otherwise and kept mum.

In fifteen minutes they emptied the whisky and they finished

---

[1] Subhas Chandra Bose would have been amused to hear himself described as Boshji. He was known to be in Nazi Germany.

off the beer (despite persistent invitation I stood by absolutely dry). And in came the luncheon. I needn't bother you with that memorable afternoon's menu but out of courtesy to our chef from Calicut I must put on record his most marvellous performance that day. It was indeed a gourmet's dinner. Again, despite pressing invitation I resisted the temptation to share with my self-imposed guests, who polished off the dishes. It was 4.30 (thank God, the terrace was cooling for Jose as the shadows lengthened) and the party rose and pulled itself to attention, revolvers back in their holsters.

Then they invited me to go for a drive them. Suppressing my panic I put on a clean pair of pants and got ready to be taken for a ride, in old gangster fashion. But first they searched me, my clothes as well as my anatomy. Then I walked down to the street flanked by two soldiers on either side. I squeezed into the middle of the rear seat with armed escorts on either side and the Jeep sped off. Except for Japanese staff cars and Jeeps the streets were deserted. We swung off Middle Road into Selegie Road and then into Stamford Road, where the old YMCA building is located. I had my emotions under pretty good control up to the moment it struck me that I was being taken to the dreaded Kempeitai headquarters. Rumour had infested that building with the most horrible stories. Tales of torture that only the Japanese were capable of. A split second before the Jeep shot past the gates of that ominous building I passed out, my escorts staring ahead as if nothing had happened. When I came around I thanked my birthday luck and composed myself, straightening and squeezing my shoulders between my escorts. We sped along the Esplanade, swerved past Fullerton Building and stopped in front of the Netherlands Trading Society building off Raffles Place. I could not fathom what dragons lurked inside. Throughout our fifteen-minute ride, not a word was spoken to me but my new-found acquaintances whispered to each other in Nippon-go, so much so that I began to fear the worst.

Blind panic seized me again as I allowed myself to be escorted up the stairs to the second floor, after of course another thorough personal check. We moved on and came to a halt before a highly polished teak door on the third floor. The bell was rung and a *tampi* came out and inspected us, then he unlocked the door. We entered a reception room and my escorts went into another room. They returned almost immediately after submitting the latest additions to the John dossier. I sat on a bench in the reception room while the person in the *sanctum sanctorum* presumably read through the dossier. My escorts vanished without a word. The Indian *tampi*, brought from Alor Star, as I discovered later, had been taught not to talk. After about fifteen minutes during which I was almost sick with fear, the bell rang. I was ushered into an elegantly furnished room. There was an otherworldly feeling in the air. The man – let us call him Sato[2] for brevity – spoke perfect King's English. About thirty, he was an Economics tripos from Cambridge University.

---

2 This and other Japanese names that follow are purely fictitious except in the case of well-known personalities like Count Terauchi, Yamashita, etc.

Sato: 'Let's cut short the formalities. We know exactly what you were doing on the *Tribune* before the war. You know little of the history of your copy after you pass it down to the press. We have before us incontrovertible evidence to prove you were the author of three bitterly anti-Japanese leading articles last November. So let's cut out any apologies. Do you want to work for us? If not ... I leave it to your discretion. Well, we're not to rely on your pen to drive the British back to their isles. You have your choice; take it or leave it. What have you to say?'

They wanted me to work for them: The sweet realisation brought tears to my eyes as I told him: 'I'm willing to join you in whatever capacity you want me to. Pardon me please, for whatever I had done while under the British.'

'Yes, you may join us tomorrow. Your office will be on the first floor of this building.'

'I shall report for duty tomorrow. Thanks very much.'

'You have your life in your own hands, not mine.'

'I quite understand. Goodbye.'

I was shaking like a leaf as I went down the stairs. The Jeep was still waiting, and the Japanese soldiers immediately flew up the stairs to get their orders. In an instant they hastened down and ceremoniously escorted me to the rear seat of the Jeep. The armed men stood down while the other sat by the driver and we drove back to Middle Road – and we did not go by the old YMCA.

Remember, it was my birthday. What a lot had happened, and what a lot did not! Wasn't I hungry? But it had to be subordinated to the eventful moment. The story sped through our neighbourhood that I had been taken to the Kempeitai for 'questioning'. Shonan well knew what this meant. And practically the entire Malayalee community in the area called at my flat. An ardent Seventh Day Adventist was about to say a prayer when the Japanese soldier who was with me knocked at my door to let us in. The door flew open, and the soldier presented me to the small assemblage, roughly thirty men. Tears flowed profusely all round, and the inscrutable Japanese soldier left.

Krishna made some porridge, and would allow me to speak only after I had my belly full. Jose was too excited to speak; he merely looked on with tearful eyes. Well, by about 8pm everybody had left, leaving us to plan our future. I do not believe in astrology. So, I seldom look into a life-chart of mine written on palm leaves hidden away back at my home in Travancore. My astrologer, or the *kanian,* had forecast a five-year void in my life after I turned 35. In later years when I was shown this chart at home I so badly wanted to reward this astrologer but he was dead.

Jose and I talked softly, almost whispered, until about midnight when we turned in after chanting – no, whispering – my favourite hymn, *Abide With Me.*

Poor Aladdin had at long last found the Magic Lamp of survival in Shonan, or so it seemed to me at the time. I was determined not to lose it at whatever cost. I went to sleep, faintly aware that all would be well with us from the morrow.

9

Willing Slave

AT THE TIME, Jose and I were practically inseparable. He being totally green to Singapore as well as its native language, Malay, we were thrown on each other's company ever since the Japanese reached Singapore. Therefore, Jose got ready to accompany me as I left for Raffles Place on the morning of April 22 in response to Sato's instructions. We were about to leave when a car pulled up in front of our flat. The driver came up and said he was to take me to the office. Warily, I confided in him a secret. 'May I not bring my brother along for an interview with Mr Sato?' After a brief pause, he replied in the affirmative, but added as an aside: 'Mister ... too much of the West. In Nippon we say "san".' Then he sat down by my disconnected, sealed radio, and minutely observed it had never been used for illegal operations. As it later turned out, he was an expert radio engineer who specialised in his craft, first in America and then in Germany, now attached to Domei. His broken English, too, was deliberate. Though not a *Nisei* (second-generation Japanese settled in the US or Canada), he spoke fluent English, as I later discovered. His name was Ko Nagai who later turned out to be one of my best friends. He left for Leyte in the

Philippines towards the end of 1943. After the war I heard he had fallen in Corregidor.

As we climbed the stairs, I heard Nagai asking somebody if Sato-san was in his room on the first floor. It was only then that I realised it was not San Sato, but the other way round. Luckily for me, Senkichi Sato, Chief of Shonan Bureau of Domei Tusin Sya (news agency), was knee-deep in office files, and directed me to a door with the name-board 'ENGLISH SECTION: Mr Namoru Iwanaga'. As we entered the room, Sato said something in Nippon-go to the man under whom I was to work until redemption. Iwanaga welcomed me with a beaming smile, and admonished me:

'Well, we have a full report before us on what you had been doing before the war. If you will work for Domei we are ready to forget your antecedents. Remember, the Kempeitai pardoned you because you have your wife and four children now in India. You wouldn't be standing before me now if the Kempeitai hadn't given you the benefit of the doubt. I can tell you in confidence that we will shortly be moving to India, your motherland. You know Mr Subhas Chandra Bose is in Axis hands now, and might eventually appear in Shonan. Would you move with him to India with thousands of others who will be trained and equipped by Nippon?'

With emphasis I declared 'yes'. Thereupon he rang for his *tampi* and asked him to bring a chair. After I had sat down, he told me of Japanese plans to pour into India, through Manipur, a quarter million armed Indians led by Bose who, he again and again emphasised, would be known as 'Nataji'[1]. He continued:

'If we find that your pen can shoot better than a rifle, we might dissuade you from joining the Nataji's army. Otherwise, you will be cannon fodder like any other soldier.'

I replied only future events could prove where I might be more effective, on the battlefield or at the editorial desk. 'To be frank,' I added, 'I feel it my duty to march with my countrymen to my motherland if ever I get an opportunity to do so.'

We shook hands, and that settled my future. Iwanaga outlined what I was to do and gave me a sheaf of Domei cables and a bunch of reference books. I pretended to be eagerly studying the cables but what was uppermost in my mind was Jose who lingered on the veranda. A little while later I went to Iwanaga's desk and told him of my personal troubles. Jose, too, was immediately engaged. I went out and brought him in. I gave him a chair near mine, and we appeared to be hard at study. But in my mind I was already in a jungle track in the Arakans on India's north-eastern border. It was not artillery fire that resounded in my ears but the gentle, sonorous *Jana Gana Mana*, our National Anthem, accompanied by soft flute, violin, and a softer drum. At the time, I never could believe anybody in India would shoot at us. Would ever gunfire shatter the lilting *Jana Gana Mana* on Indian soil?

As the years slip by I reluctantly join the crowds that believe Netaji had disappeared behind the curtain. Yet, not only to me but to millions of my countrymen the Netaji is an immortal symbol.

---

1 'Neta' in Sanskrit means 'leader' and 'ji' is an honorific suffix.

He will remain so as long as the torch of freedom burns in India.

My brother and I lingered in Shonan's Domei House till noon when we were asked to have luncheon with the rest of the Japanese staff. It was quite filling. The emphasis was on fish, not on meat. Raw fish with a hot sauce was the only dish we backed out of. We answered as best we could a thousand questions on the steamroller driver that razed Singapore sooner than they expected, and at one we were back at our desk.

I was asked to help secure a dozen subeditors and fast typists down to bicycle-*tampi*s. We picked our men and women from the thousands who called at Domei. And we were ready for action within a week.

The office car took us to Domei every morning, and returned us to our home in the evening. The was indeed a very great privilege those days when barristers, doctors, engineers and former civil servants, not to mention ex-towkays, were trudging the streets. And I knew many who dismissed us as quislings[2]. For myself, I knew what I was collaborating in, and why.

It was the job of the English section to subedit Domei cables from Tokyo, and distribute about fifty cyclostyled copies to newspapers, the broadcasting station and various military departments. The first day or two Iwanaga closely scrutinised my subbed copy as well as the cyclostyled copies before they were distributed. As we progressed Iwanaga became a mere presence in

---

2 The word originates from the Norwegian war-time leader Vidkun Quisling who was head of a collaborationist regime in Norway during the Second World War.

our office to whom only such Japanese words whose meanings we did not know were referred for interpretation.

I knew I was still suspect. I didn't know why at first, but gradually it dawned on me that it was because of my name, or rather the fact that Churchill and I worshipped the same God. The Japanese could hardly believe that a Christian like me would ever fight Churchill's Empire. The opinion of most Japanese on Domei was that I was trying to hoodwink them by painting over my red, white and blue the Indian green, white, and saffron. But the question asked by other Japanese on my behalf, including my first day's acquaintance, Ko Nagai, was: Weren't Christians fighting on Nippon's side? There were hundreds of Japanese Christians, other than the *Nisei*, fighting in all the three services. The question was left unanswered for the time being.

Sato summoned Iwanaga and myself for a chat in the second week of May. The chief told me I had progressed much further than they expected and – to my utter surprise – asked me if I could take charge of the daily 1,000-word broadcast beamed at India. I said I would do my best. After the first broadcast was released there was a rush on Iwanaga's office as his co-workers from throughout the building, one after the other, went to thank him and congratulate him for having discovered *John*. By the way, it was the Apostle Thomas who was reputed to have earned such a celebrated sobriquet – another John, another time. This *John*, the *Indo-jin* (son of India) had a different mission: Indian independence. Those who have studied the history of the Indian National Congress, the main engine of the independence movement, ought to know that among the millions in our part of India who still call themselves St Thomas Christians, there were patriots like George Joseph who spent years in British Indian jails during the civil disobedience campaigns. It is symptomatic of the times that among Indian intelligentsia you could find hardly a single one who differentiates patriotism on linguistic or religious lines. All are represented in India's fighting services, Hindus, Muslims, Christians, Parsis, the former untouchables, etc. The very name Christian struck most Japanese as somewhat obnoxious. But in my case eventually the Japanese were compelled to admit that patriotism could hardly be a sole predicate of one's religion.

Those were indeed stirring days. The Samurai seemed drunk with power. His internal squabbles over, the Samurai was lording it over South Asia, one foot bogged down in the mire of an unyielding China and the other entrenched in the old East Indies. One could picture the snarling ogre firing a revolver non-stop at the Chinese dragon and holding a sword in the other hand dripping with British, American and Dutch blood. Anyone who got in the Samurai's way paid in blood. There was a marked cooling in the war as everyone paused to take stock of the new realities. American and British forces needed time to rebuild and resupply after the Pearl Harbour sneak attack that destroyed many of America's finest fighting ships, and Britain's ouster from the European mainland. General Douglas MacArthur, driven out of the Philippines, bided his time in the East while General Eisenhower marshalled his forces in the West for a full-frontal attack on the Germans. Storm clouds were gathering once more with cyclonic force. The reality in Asia was that the Japanese had been attacking China with everything in their arsenal for over five years. The more the Japanese decimated China, the more Chinese heads popped up over the bunker. The bloodletting had come to a stalemate and it appeared as if the Samurai might have to look elsewhere. The conquest and acquisition of Manchuria in 1930 had failed to deliver China's riches, eventually driving Japan into the Axis camp. And when the United States enforced an embargo on the export of strategic raw materials to Japan, it became clear that sooner or later Japan would be compelled to move south in search of those supplies. She did, and she was, at the time of which I write, mistress of the Pacific. And more. Apart from posing a direct threat to the Australian mainland by bombing Darwin and fighting southward in New Guinea, Japan was scanning the horizon for a loophole through which the Netaji could '*Challo Dilli*!' Indian PoWs[3] were allowed to enter the city freely. But there were some Indian soldiers unenthusiastic about the Netaji and they were behind bars. Yet, in the event, practically 95 per cent of Indian PoWs joined in the would-be march to Delhi, beaten back in the Arakans in Burma by Mountbatten's South East Asia Command (SEAC).

After four or five weeks of my broadcasts to India, Sato sent a note to me through Iwanaga saying Domei had received a special commendation from Nazi propaganda chief Heinrich Himmler

---

[3] They were not prisoners but soldiers without an army for the time being.

upon 'our brilliant effort' and urged me to continue the good work. I did not know how to react. A 'well done' from Himmler is not something one is proud of except that it shows admiration for the skill and technique in selling a message. I was not happy about Himmler's intrusion into my life but I kept my mouth shut and my neck intact. When I returned to Calcutta in 1946 I was told my broadcasts from Shonan were printed in Bengal and widely distributed by Leftists of the day. They were more pro-Indian than being anti-British. At the time of the Great Bengal Famine (1942-1943) I warned Delhi it was unfair and cruel that tens of thousands of British in India were battening on the fat of the land while millions of famished Indians dropped dead on pavements, obstructing the passage of well-fed nabobs from Sussex or Edinburgh – their pockets chock-full of maharanis – to Calcutta's cabarets. Didn't they trip over the corpses? Watch it, Netaji is on the march to Calcutta! Millions of people from all over India are moving north-eastward to welcome their leader from abroad. So I went on, day after day, plastering the British with verbal gunfire.

Lord Wavell was apprised of this wordy barrage levelled at him from old Singapore. So was SEAC. There was a lot of conjecture about the author of those 'dirty fulminations' from Shonan. Although I was fairly unknown in India's officialdom, the Criminal Investigations Department discovered that a Christian named John had worked on a newspaper in Singapore and that he had not returned home. They found that I was from the old native State of Travancore, then moved quickly to establish my father's and my wife's addresses[4]. They also set up a line of inquiries to discover whether my father or my wife received any money from outside India.

My old friend and colleague, Mr Edwin Glover of the *Tribune*, was then in India, assisting in SEAC's Publicity Section. He knew I hadn't returned to India. Through his representations in London, Reuter sent five hundred rupees to my wife, a welcome gift for which I record my heartfelt gratitude to Reuter and Mr Glover. To a SEAC query he couldn't say what I might do while under the Japanese in Shonan. Sir (latterly, meekly, Dr) CP Ramaswami Iyer was then Dewan (Governor) of Travancore. His police were receiving typed copies of my daily broadcasts. By coincidence, way back in 1934 I had had the privilege of being received by Sir and Lady CP at their medieval looking mansion in Mylapore, Madras. The reason: My wife's father, Mr CJ Joshua, was a university physical education instructor in Trivandrum, the state capital, and he used to provide gymnastic lessons and exercise routines to the brilliant barrister whenever he visited. And he visited often because he was legal adviser to the Syrian Church in a bitter lawsuit that lasted more than thirty-five years. All that was well before Shonan. I do not know if Sir CP knew the identity of the 'John' the Travancore police had been asked to apprehend if ever 'John' turned up. I did visit the state in 1947 – but I was tipped off that the police were after me. I departed the country quickly

---

4 My wife Annie and four children were living with her parents in Trichur, in the then Cochin state.

and returned to Singapore, a different island trying to shake off the heat of *wasabi* and the taste of *sashimi*.

Come, step back into my time machine and let's go back to Shonan. Iwanaga called me in one day and told me my salary was two hundred military dollars a month.

'Don't be sorry, John-san, we'll see all found,' he said. 'You wouldn't be left in the lurch.'

I was asked to send my servant to a military depot to collect rations for three every week. The following week I heard that CID men in civilian clothes were on guard duty outside my flat day and night. Now that I had 'food for three' and transport, life was fairly comfortable for us. It goes without saying that we gave away to neighbours whatever we could spare.

In due course I discovered that the question came up before Sato whether I could be better utilised as editor of the *Azad Hind*. Iwanaga strongly favoured my continuance as his No. 2 at Domei while my old friend, Sivaram[5] was to be editor of the *Azad Hind*, designed as the Indian community's mouthpiece. When I revisited Malaya in 1963 Sivaram had resurfaced as editor of *The Malayan Times* in Kuala Lumpur, and Leslie Hoffman, newly elevated to Dato then Tan Sri by Malaysia's King, was Editor-in-Chief of the Straits Times Group in Singapore and Malaysia. Tan Sri Hoffman, who had worked with me on the *Tribune*, had bounced back from the 90 lb bag of bones that came out of detention by the Kempeitai in 1942. Khoo Teng Soon, who became Managing Editor of *The*

---

5 Author of a bestseller in India, *Challo Dilli*.

Straits Times, was also an old colleague from the *Tribune*. I met him at his desk in 1963.

Before long the Japanese gave me full responsibility for the work of the English Section. After Netaji's arrival in Singapore I was allowed to read and digest English translations of broadcasts from Berlin, Rome, Warsaw and Prague. A few weeks later I saw a soldier deliver to Iwanaga a massive bundle of cyclostyled sheets with the instruction 'For John-san's attention'. Iwanaga, who was still at his Domei desk because of his other unnamed duties, immediately sent the bundle of paper to me with a note that said, 'To be read only by you, and then return to Iwanaga-san. Must not be left unattended.' Then London! New York! Until the end of 1943 I had the privilege of reading what the BBC and CBS said the previous day. But later I was told the BBC had ceased functioning following a Luftwaffe raid on London. I had no way of verifying this. Was this deliberate blackout of unpalatable news? Was the war going so disastrously bad for Germany while, at the same time, MacArthur's island-hopping was bringing him within bombing range of the Japanese home islands? About the end of September 1943 there was a sudden and prolonged power blackout in Singapore's harbour area. An Indian port worker told me that some ships had been scuttled, nobody knew why or how. I could see there was some 'loss of face' for the Japanese. It was many years before I heard of the sensational *Operation Jaywick* raid from Australia in which seven Japanese ships were sunk in the outer roads (shipping channels) of Singapore harbour. For the hapless people of Shonan *Jaywick* was the first hint that the British were still alive and kicking. But the Netaji's arrival was imminent and Indians in Shonan were worked up to a frenzy. Couldn't we sing through to India?

10

The First Murders

BY THE LAST quarter of 1942 practically every trading house in Shonan was reopened, trade or no trade. Those shops and businesses whose owners could not be traced were occupied by Nippon-jin entrepreneurs who did whatever business that came their way, their main preoccupation being the Kempeitai's watchdogs. All their expenses were met by the military administration, and they fattened their pockets with what they could squeeze from Chinese commercial interests. The average Japanese looked out for a good foreign watch, camera, rings, studs, etc for himself and ornaments, perfume, muslin scarves, cosmetics for his wife and geisha acquaintances. All paid for in military currency. Just as a memento he might keep a few thousand-dollar Straits dollar notes. If such notes happened to fall within sight of any Japanese they had to be handed over at par with Japanese military notes, which, by and by, slumped to well beneath the gutter. But backed by Japanese guns, the military scrip went a long way in Shonan markets which sold Japanese or local produce such as greens, eggs, fish and poultry. Military prices and military notes did not extend to such things as whisky, beer, cigarettes, tweeds and shoes.

They were in the black market, available only in Straits currency – or in equivalent cartloads of banana[1] notes.

I was once present at a black market transaction in a back alley in Chinatown. A Chinese go-between contacted a Japanese buyer who was willing to pay the price in Straits dollars for some bottles of scotch. The go-between wanted us to be at a specified spot in Chinatown about seven in the evening. As we branched off from South Bridge Road into the area vaguely defined as Chinatown I had an eerie feeling of trespassing on communal preserves. And Kurasawa, on whose insistence I had accompanied him on this potentially disastrous adventure, sat by me nursing his revolver in a side pocket. Chinatown was bursting with humanity, good, bad and the indifferent. Piercing eyes, men's as well women's, bored into us as the car sped to our encounter with the go-between. The man we sought sat cross-legged on the five-footway. Without a word he got into the car and squeezed himself into the rear seat. He instructed the driver and we proceeded by a devious route to an opium den, half a mile away. At the door of this establishment six bottles of what appeared to be whisky and a tin of imported cigarettes suddenly appeared. Eighty-eight dollars was the price plus twelve for himself, a neat hundred. The exchange was quick. The man had hardly time to check the watermarks on the old British notes than we were speeding away. They were genuine, I was assured, otherwise assassinations could be expected.

---

1 So called because Japanese military notes had banana trees on one side stating the value.

At the *sukiyaki*[2] party in Domei House on Feb 15, 1943, first anniversary of the Greater East Asia Co-Prosperity Sphere, I was the only man to silently congratulate the Chinese go-between; his whisky tasted more like *samsu*, the Chinese liquor brewed from fermented rice. Whatever it was, the party went off with an Oriental swing. Roughly fifty Japanese were the hosts and the guests were two Indians, two Ceylonese, two Eurasians and a Filipino. A Chinese girl waited on each guest, her duty was to over-feed the guest and lubricate him with tumbler after tumbler of *sake*, the Japanese rice wine. If you touched your *sake* the girl would instantly refill the tumbler. It would still be full when you said *sayonara* to your hosts. Out of courtesy to our hosts, we seven had to stand up and say in unison that the party was most unforgettable. A bit humiliating, I thought, but we had to tolerate that sort of arrogance to survive. The *sake* had gone to our heads and we tottered down to the official cars, a symbol of our official untouchability. We sped past innumerable sentries and each one was dropped home. I fell asleep almost immediately, thinking of my other home and family.

Every acquaintance of mine asked me the following morning, 'How was the raw fish? I replied that the *sashimi* had come by my plate but I had given it the go-by. I might try it some other time. To be frank, Japanese culinary art is far inferior to that of the Chinese who would cook anything from termites to tortoises

---

[2] A popular Japanese hot-pot dish. There were unfamiliar ingredients in it.

and make them inviting and tasty. Maybe Chinese cuisine is older. Nippon cook for Nippon-jin, not for anyone else.

Japanese who would not touch a mango for some perceived poison, might for days follow a dangerous snake for its liver which, eaten raw, is a rare delicacy with them. Before Japanese troops sailed from Hainan for the Malayan campaign each man was given a confidential note entitled, *Read this alone – and the war can be won*.[3] The following excerpts are taken from it:

'If you discover a dangerous snake, you must of course kill it. You should also swallow its liver, and cook the meat. There is no better medicine for strengthening the body.'

'When eating mangoes, do not drink milk (goat's milk) or spirits at the same time.'

I am glad the Japanese had not forbidden the consumption of mangoes except when accompanied by goat's milk and spirits. When there were no more snakes to chase, and skirts disappeared completely from public view, idleness began to affect the occupiers. Japanese of all classes resorted to crime. Despite severe punishment meted out to those caught, some Japanese troops raided outlying kampongs. Women were raped and shops looted. And quite a few Japanese officers and men were caught and severely punished. I quote the English translation of another fiat to the army:

'If you look at the history of past campaigns you will see that troops who are really efficient in battle do not plunder and rob,

---

[3] This pamphlet was translated by CW Sargent, Department of Oriental Studies, University of Sydney.

chase after women, or dink and quarrel. When a hero of many campaigns is court-martialled for plunder or rape, and finds himself sentenced to several years of penal servitude, there is no excuse. This is a warning that should be particularly heeded by those who are in camp after the battle, or are assigned to duties in the rear, far from the sound of explosions. Not to heed it is to invite a failure which can never be lived down.' Still, Japanese cruelty of the time makes one wonder whether there was any basis to their avowed faith in Buddhism whose cardinal tenet is compassion.

There is the story of an elderly Asian doctor practising in Johore Bharu, just across the Causeway from Singapore. The war had broken out when he was about to close his clinic and go into retirement. He cancelled his ocean voyage and remained at his post attending to his large and growing clientele. Thousands of young Chinese who had taken to the jungle to escape the Japanese were still out there, and they were all branded Communists. A detective reported to the Japanese that the doctor was selling drugs to the Communists and making a fortune in Straits dollars. A detachment of soldiers surrounded the doctor's home when he returned about 11 after a long day. The 59-year-old doctor – to spare feelings in many quarters I cannot disclose his name – and his wife, 49, and their four children were said to have been subjected to what was described to me as 'gruelling examination' until the following morning. When dawn came all six were taken to the garden behind their home and ordered to dig their own grave. The Samurai sword did its work. An informant told me that the bodies were left uncovered in their shallow graves for two days as 'festering lesson to the underlings of Communists'.

Another story – for the sake of our conscience let's label it a mere story and let's call them the McElwies – relates to a Singapore Eurasian family that moved in with a cousin in a rubber estate in Selangor when the city was bombed in December 1941. Within weeks of their arrival in the estate they heard that the Japanese steamroller had bypassed them and moved south to Gemas. Within weeks the British had surrendered and the McElwies discovered that a small Japanese picket had been posted about two furlongs from the estate gates. Soon soldiers with a faint smattering of English words started visiting the McElwies and showed off their linguistic prowess. One soldier, about 20, was enthralled by a McElwie girl. The Singapore McElwies comprised of Christopher, 60, his wife Joan, 53, and their children Francis, 31, his wife Isabella, 23, Alex, 26, Arthur, 20, Mary, 17, and Margarette, 10. The Selangor McElwies were Matthias, 40, his wife Anne, 32, and their three sons, Vincent, nine, Tom, seven, and Winston, three.

Christopher was by nature of a retiring and modest temperament. He seldom went out even for an evening stroll. Whenever he was not at his crossword puzzle or reading detective stories the old man would sometimes come out to play with the bouncing youngsters in the garden. 'Damn' was the strongest word Christopher ever uttered but he was now wont to mutter the expletive once or twice to the Japanese Hamlet who came to the McElwies home almost every evening. Often the Japanese soldier was accompanied by lesser lights, also in uniform and fully armed. It was evident on the first day that he had his eye on the fair Mary. He plied the McElwies with canned food, cigarettes and sweets.

On a Saturday evening Hamlet came over with four comrades. On entering the drawing room he displayed to his hosts a jar of *sake* and by some mimicry conveyed to his hosts that he and his party were hungry. Some sort of a meal was hastily prepared and all sat down to dinner. Hamlet was beginning to soliloquise for 'Maaaaaarrie' when the shy girl, with head bent, was escorted into the room by her mother. Hamlet rose and touched the girl's arm and said something in a jumbled medley of broken English and Nippon-go. He motioned the girl to sit on the arm of his chair. Christopher, who had hovered in the background, came into view and the sight that he beheld was this Japanese brute pawing his daughter. He drew out a revolver from his pocket and shot the soldier at point blank range. The other four fled the room. Three stood guard outside the house while the fourth ran to his picket. Japanese infantry arrived and surrounded the ill-fated McElwie bungalow. Its thirteen occupants were killed by the Samurai sword (not shot, as a measure of economy) and the bungalow razed to the ground. The soldier's body was cremated and his ashes sent to his home in Japan while the thirteen Eurasian bodies were exposed to public view for twenty-hours before they were buried – in graves that the victims themselves had dug.

There were many similar tales of Japanese heroism in the face of unarmed civilians. Little wonder that the entire occupied territory remained as quiet as a morgue. People struggled day and night to find a morsel of food. Whatever rice was brought from Thailand and Indo-China passed through Japanese hands, not through private traders. Not a grain of rice was available in the markets. The Japanese gave rations only to those who worked for them. Others were labelled 'queen bees' and they had to fend for themselves. Luckily the economic life-blood of the country began to come on stream. Tapping of rubber trees and dredging of tin mines revived and strategic raw materials began to be stockpiled in Yokohama. Apparently Japan's military might reached its zenith in 1942.

From early 1943 we began to hear of Bose's dramatic escape from Calcutta and of his arrival in Berlin. Later it was announced from Tokyo that he would come to Shonan. That was dynamite for Indians. People besieged the Domei office for more news on the great Indian nationalist and patriot. He was called Netaji from the day he landed in Shonan. Birth pangs of Independent India had begun – blood-curdling and confusing. Will she emerge as one country, or several? The immediate distress in occupied Singapore was instantly forgotten by every Indian as their eyes glazed over at the thought of the glittering future of a liberated India. 'Let's march to Delhi' reverberated all over the island in Tamil, Hindi, Telugu, Malayalam and any other Indian language you can think of. '*Challo Dilli*' became a general greeting that replaced 'Hello'.

Irrespective of caste, creed or colour the entire Indian community as well as Indian PoWs rose to the cry of '*Challo Dilli*' all over the island. Labourers marched with what the British called the white-collar clerical classes, men, women and children shouting slogans in a babel of languages but the goal was the same everywhere – freedom. Hitherto they had only heard of Gandhi's salt *satyagraha*[4], his non-violence campaign, his fasts-unto-death and his 'Quit India' cry that achieved insignificant results. But here in Shonan was an opportunity to raise an Indian National Army to shoot its way back to India. Netaji spoke to crowds made up of workmen, clerks, petty merchants, lawyers, doctors, artisans and rubber tappers that force was the only language the British understood. Barristers such as SC Goho, KP Kesava Menon (later editor of an influential daily in Kerala), N Raghavan and John Thivy (both of whom became envoys when India became independent in 1947) were some of the Indian leaders in Malaya and Shonan during the last war. Few outside Malaya and Singapore know the extent of financial aid that the independence movement received from Nattukottai Chettiars (traditional money-lenders from South India) or their agents overseas. Like the Quakers, they are most frugal in habiliments as well as food but when it came to the need to assist the Netaji's war effort the Chettiar community unfastened their purse-strings and contributed most liberally. Every Indian man and woman[5] threw his or her mite into Netaji's war chest. Tragically, the great INA push into Assam was a failure. Many men and women died, but it delivered a salutary message: India achieved independence two years after Hirohito's surrender.

---

4 Campaign against a cruel British tax on salt. *Satyagraha* means a non-violent search for truth.
5 Mostly jewellery.

As 1942 came to a close practically none but the very wealthy could subsist except by working for the Japanese. Each worker had at least a dozen dependents and it was indeed a miracle how the population filled its belly each day. Malaya, and I include Singapore in that name at this time, was one of the few Asian nations that had never known the pangs of hunger and famine. And because the Japanese realised that their entire war effort would be undermined if the civilian population became desperate enough to fight back, avenues of employment were doubled and trebled to provide what was known as 'rice-jobs' for anyone willing to work. It was still hard work, the Japanese overseer would work with their men until the day's task was finished. To borrow a Chinese metaphor made famous in the Sixties, a hundred flowers had to bloom where none did before[6]. Whatever the job, the Japanese went the whole hog leaving nothing to chance. Women in the occupied territories also made a grain of rice go the distance of hundred.

---

6 Mao used the metaphor in relation to political thought.

11

Lovely Penang

THAT THE JAPANESE were a most courteous people, typical of the proverbial peace, tranquillity and compassion of the Orient was generally accepted the world over until 1930 when they annexed Manchuria. They just marched in and took over without fanfare. The very name Manchuria was trimmed (again, very quietly) to evolve a new name signifying the change in leadership – 'Manchukuo'. The lone survivor of the Manchu Dynasty, Prince Henry Pu-yi, was not in captivity, it was explained with tongue in cheek. He had been moved, compassionately, to a larger palace more in keeping with the dignity of the great Manchu House, protected by Imperial Guards from Tokyo. To avoid unhealthy contamination, the Prince was kept as far away from the people as possible. With Manchuria in her hands, it was comparatively easy for Japan to extend the fighting to China proper five or six years later. Although riven with internecine feuds, China or rather small parts of China vigorously resisted Japan, engaging her in a ding-dong battle, until Japan was forced to look elsewhere for the quick victories that were so indispensable to her.

These, in a nutshell, were the antecedents to Japan's southward drive. Those Western diplomats and businessmen who intimately knew the Japanese before the outbreak of the Pacific War were well aware the Japanese wouldn't bite unless bitten. The West did not view the effects upon Japan of the stoppage of iron, rubber and oil exports from the United States and Britain with the gravity it warranted. Like the British the Japanese are an insular people anxious to trade with the rest of the world on level terms. And unlike the British, who had vast colonial possessions in Asia and Africa, the Japanese who were essentially asleep until the Meiji Restoration[1] had to find not only raw materials but markets as well to sustain her growing economy. By the time Japan was ready to make contact with the outside world, Asia and Africa had already been parcelled out among Western Powers. What would Japan's industry do if shut out from world markets?

Japan did what any other nation would have done in the circumstances – allying herself with the Axis Powers. If she were to continue as a trading nation Japan had somehow or other to have access to raw materials she so badly lacked. In the circumstances, it is manifestly absurd to say that Pearl Harbour or Singapore was totally unexpected. Those who diligently followed day-to-day events in 1940 and 1941 would only be amazed why Japan had not entered the arena earlier. She was indeed driven to the wall, nay, flattened against the wall.

---

1 A chain of events that restored practical imperial rule in 1868 under Emperor Meiji. It led to enormous changes in Japan's political and social structure and nationalism responsible for the emergence of Japan as a modernised, although militarist, nation in the early 20th Century.

Compared to the acute mental agony the Japanese nation as a whole went through when denied imports of vital strategic materials, Hiroshima and Nagasaki were mere child's play. The atom bombs merely gave them an opportunity to surrender; it meant the survival of the Japanese people to this day. Otherwise the entire land and its people, who are the greatest non-nuclear power in world commerce, would have been extinct in this year of grace 1979. With crushed heels, Japan limped into the arena. There were few in Washington or war-torn London in 1940-1941 who could read correctly the real import of Japan's growing taciturnity. The West merely dismissed it as inscrutable.

I had a somewhat close association with Japanese newspapermen, some of whom were quite brilliant English language scholars, for more than three years. Our relationship never exceeded the bounds of formality. Except in the case of one solitary instance, namely, in that of Nagai-san who led the armed soldiers in the raid on my Middle Road flat and to whom I owe my life, I had not been of more than nodding acquaintance with most Japanese who appeared to be rather frigid. When everything went according to schedule, the Japanese like everybody else were nice to get along with. But like children everywhere they were extremely morose when anything went awry. Early in 1943 the Japanese Navy had a bitter mauling in the Coral Sea, and as usual we were getting Everest-high puffs from Tokyo of how America's Pacific Fleet had been blown out of the ocean at an undisclosed point. As remnants of the Japanese fleet limped back into safe waters we of the news agency fraternity became aware that the

Americans were coming back after all, and that Pearl Harbor was not the end, as Japan first imagined.

About this time the Americans, whom the Axis had earlier dismissed as past praying for, were preparing the groundwork for their island-hopping strategy in the Pacific which was later to blossom forth in the occupation of the Philippines and then of Okinawa. Still the Japanese held out until Hiroshima and Nagasaki (August 1945) when Emperor Hirohito, who had neither constitutional nor traditional right to make a decision or even to express an opinion without Cabinet consent, took the issue in his own hands by declaring, 'To stop the war on this occasion is the only way to save the nation from destruction ... I decide this war shall be stopped.' That reset the stage for a new class of actors. The Japanese merchant kow-tows in, and exeunt the old Junta.

Why were the Japanese so cruel to those whom they adjudged to be against their war effort? For more than three years before the Pacific War, Japan had been involved in what she then termed the 'China incident'. Could there be any war between blood-brothers? So China remained a mere 'incident' in the eyes of the nation that first precipitated it. Early in 1943 Nagai-san spoke to me of the fortunes of the China 'incident':

'Whatever you may call it, war or incident, the operation in China was an enigma. You fight northward for days, and then comes the enemy from the south. And when the fighting moves eastward and you annihilate everything before you until you touch the seashore, then arise Chinese hordes in your rear. Wherever you move in China keep an eye ahead and turn the other behind.

Good we moved south, eh?'

I replied: 'Oh, China? A welcome riddance indeed. Aren't we[2] freer now? With our troops now in the Moluccas and Burma, we stand as a perpetual threat to Australia and British India. And the Americans haven't yet recovered from Pearl Harbour.'

Nagai: 'John-san, the worm has begun to turn at last. The Americans shot at our navy, and we suffered some losses. The reason for our unusually long faces, of which you remarked the other day, was a disaster in the Coral Sea.'

It was soon heard in the office that Nagai and I were to leave for Penang at the earliest. And at the end of February 1943, Nagai and I, accompanied by my bosom friend Bhoy Kar left for Penang by train. We were on a mission to start a Domei network reaching up to the north-eastern borders of India, that is, preparing the groundwork for Netaji Bose.

En route to Penang, we planned to spend a day at Kuala Lumpur where Domei already had a bureau. On alighting at the station about 11.30 at night, we telephoned the local bureau for two cars which were immediately sent to us.

Nagai let us have one car with its Malay syce until the following morning. While our Japanese associate drove up to Domei, we asked our syce to take us to a friend's home in Bukit Istana. I soon noticed that few people could be seen at the railway station, and none on the streets. We felt a bit uneasy but our big armbands bearing in Nippon-go the word DOMEI followed by

---

2 Only way of speaking in the 'us' or 'them' language.

the legend that we are Indians gave us a lot of confidence.

As the car turned into Bangsar Road, there was an unearthly shout from a roadside hut. The poor Malay driver stopped the car and we got out and approached the sentry (that was what it was), our arms up in meek submission. I thought the huge Domei insignia on the side of our car would have been enough. Far from it. First, he examined the car, and straightaway telephoned Domei whether their car No. XYZ was out now. Nagai's explanation ought to have placated the sentry but it gave him some sort of satisfaction to proceed with an item-by-item examination of all our personal possessions. He was very angry that a Domei employee – the legend said I was second-in-command to the chief of the English Section – couldn't speak Nippon-go. After seeing twelve genuine Japanese military dollars in my purse he relented and let us depart, our arms down.

About 2am we reached our destination, and we went to bed after a muffled conversation with our host, Dr Prasad. As soon as it was dawn, the syce took the car back to Domei, and Indians in the neighbourhood flocked to Dr Prasad's 'to have a word with the Indian newsman on Domei'. Subhas Chandra Bose was soon to arrive in Singapore but I couldn't say when. The Bengal Famine: Thousands upon thousands had perished in the streets of Calcutta, the ancient seat of British power. Their blood called out for retribution ... Asia's rice bowl was in our (Japan's) possession. How could we help Bengal now? Nothing was possible without arms and adequate manpower. Everybody's face was a question mark as the informal talk concluded. After a hasty breakfast we walked as fast as we could to reach the railway station before ten when the train to Penang was scheduled to leave.

We had a fairly uneventful journey up to Butterworth where we caught the ferry to Penang island which I was visiting for the first time. A car awaited us at the jetty, and we drove to the house in the suburbs allocated to us by the military authorities. It was night and I couldn't see the town, but as I rubbed my eyes out of bed the following morning the town appeared too good to be true. It was fairly untouched by war. As the Japanese steamroller moved down the midriff of the Malayan Peninsula, a small unit of Japanese forces had occupied this island almost without firing a single shot. It was an oasis in the Malayan desert. And as was to be expected, Chinese from all over the peninsula gradually congregated in the island.

I was quite dazzled by Penang, almost unspoilt by world tourists. It is off the beaten track. The world airlines to the Far East go either via Bangkok or Singapore. On the fifth day after the landing at Singora, Japanese planes from Phuquok island, south of Cape Cambodia, heavily bombed shipping in Georgetown Harbour. In spite of the serious damage to ships and warehouses, at the time I visited the island appeared as well as ever. The influx to Malacca of Portuguese, Spanish and later of Sir Stamford Raffles had left its successive marks also (Francis Light) on Penang, roughly three hundred miles north of Malacca. None but the British foresaw its distinct advantage as a bastion of the peninsula. It surprised everybody the British abandoned the island even before the Jitra line was written off.

The town is hardly a mile square, thickly populated by people of all ethnic backgrounds, with the upper crust living in villas on the crest or the sides of the 2,700-foot Penang Hill, which dominates the entire island. During the war, most of the Penang nabobs who couldn't get away from Singapore before the surrender were pining away in PoW camps. Therefore, most of the palatial bungalows on the hill were untenanted, barring the few occupied by high army officers. And fortunately, the Hill Railway was left intact by the British.

The Domei office was a mansion formerly occupied by a senior British civil servant. On the ground floor was the office, on the first were non-Japanese living quarters, and on the second stayed Japanese employees of Domei. Our common dining room was on the ground floor, and a Ceylonese was engaged to manage the mess. We had the pleasure of having *kopi-o* or green tea whenever called for. We had a Cantonese cook with a large retinue (alleged to be five sons, two small daughters, two wives and four grandsons). They all lived in an outhouse, and managed to apportion among themselves the entire household work, from cooking right down to general maintenance. Though the house was unguarded not a soul left our house or entered it without permission. At the farthest end of the polo ground in front of the bungalow was a thatched hut with an armed sentry day and night. But for this, we were in idyllic surroundings.

Within a week of our arrival, staff were recruited locally, office desks marshalled and newscasts prepared for distribution. On March 15, 1943, came a 'Rush' item from Shonan saying that the Kempeitai had learned that Chinese Communist elements were infiltrating Penang and other towns on the mainland, and that action would shortly be taken. As old coffee shops deteriorated to tapioca booths, with fish curry on days when the Chinese fishermen brought in a bumper catch, the mad hunt for food by those not employed in Japanese firms or government departments became all the more pressing. And in the popular frenzy few read the 'Rush' news item from Shonan with the attention it deserved.

12

Eyewitness

'OPERATION RED NETTLE' is the nearest equivalent to a Nippon-go expression meaning the liquidation of Chinese Communists. White Nettle connotes the American and the British or, as the Axis publicists often put it, Anglo–Americans. Early in 1943 the Kempeitai had secret information of a periodic influx into Penang of Red Nettles who passed off as temporary labourers at the port or as rubber tappers. They formed the spearhead of the Communist insurgents who had fled into the jungle. How did they subsist in the jungle?

Undoubtedly, they had 'contact' men in the towns all over the peninsula and in Singapore who sponged on wealthy *towkays* for 'maintaining our freedom fighters'. Naturally, the *towkays* were in an awful dilemma; neither could they pay, nor could they not pay. One in Alor Star went on paying for three months before he went broke. Not even his wife who slept with him in the same bed was aware she was sleeping with a corpse until late the following morning when the inexplicable murder (or untimely death, according to well-meaning neighbours) was reported to the Japanese. They knew who were behind the murder, and the

Kempeitai went on patiently piecing together the jigsaw puzzle. There were a number of such murders all over the country.

I don't like the Communists, or the Japanese who drove hundreds into the Communist camp. Despite several punitive expeditions by the Japanese, the Red Nettles thrived well in the jungle fastnesses from Johore right up to Kelantan in the north. Apparently, they were well provided for. Whenever they ran short of supplies such as noodles and rice, even *samsu* or tobacco, their agents contacted their sub-agents in the towns who, in turn, fleeced everybody they suspected of being wealthy. It was a vicious circle that the Japanese were determined to crush. When the Japanese demanded $50 million from the Chinese community as 'protection money', there was an accompanying promise to protect them from Communist extortion of the same kind. The military police were soon flooded with complaints that Malayans were being mulcted on the sly by Communist agents. They well knew that the entire Japanese military administration of Malaya would crumble if the Communist menace was not checked.

In our office, we got into full stride by the end of March, merrily putting out brave communiqués of Axis victories and Allied disasters. There were newscasts thrice a day. Jose and I were the only Indians on the staff, the others being mostly Chinese with a few Eurasians. After a gruelling day's work and dinner at the office mess, we retired to our living quarters about 8pm. This was the time for us to exchange the day's gossip. Except Nagai none in the office knew that Jose was my younger brother. We would concentrate upon our respective assignments and we exchanged hardly a word during office hours. Jose whispered in my ear a strange happening that came to his notice that day. Our office *amah* (maid-servant), a Chinese woman of roughly 45, had gone into town, with our manager's permission, and had returned with eleven children, most in their teens. It seems she had permission from 'above' to keep those children with her for three days. The occasion: A Chinese festival. The one room adjoining the kitchen where already more than ten of her dependents somehow existed was bloated to bursting point with this fresh consignment. There was some clever chit-chat among ourselves and we wafted aside the *amah* episode, and went to sleep.

About midnight we heard an agonised cry, muffled of course, from the more densely populated part of the town, then a harsh Japanese order. Then came more cries, though still subdued, and it went on for two or three hours. Like the other civilian residents, we sat on our beds in pitch darkness. A baby's trailing wail was carried on the wind. The town silent, the silence of terror. I murmured a prayer to save us from things that stalk by night. No one uttered a word. The occasional cry could be heard for two or three hours. In the small hours of the morning, Jose and I were benumbed to fitful sleep.

On the following morning, I met Nagai at breakfast. He thought it beneath his dignity to hail me '*Ohayo gosaimasu!*' Unlike most other Japanese, he said 'Good morning,' and I responded. There was bread (as much as we could consume) and fish-paste (no, not the awesome unbaked variety), papaya, and green tea. Pointedly, he asked:

'Had sound sleep, eh?'

'To be frank, not quite so good last night.'

'Why?'

'I was in Alice's Wonderland about 12 last night when I was almost rattled out of my sleep by an uproar from the town. I wonder what it's all about.'

Nagai replied: 'Right under the sward over which you softly tread day and night there may be serpents. Isn't it good they are destroyed before we approach our next springboard?'

'I don't quite understand.'

'We are spreading our nets far and wide to collect "nettles". If caught, they're to be destroyed in one fell sweep.'

'I see. Have many been caught?'

'If you want to, go out and see for yourself. I shall make the arrangements. Take out a car with Domei insignia.'

It was an invitation I wouldn't pass up under any circumstances. Hurriedly I got ready to be eyewitness to what might turn out to be a purge. I changed into khaki with 'Domei' emblazoned all over and with my office credentials in my breast pocket. Nagai got into touch with the Kempeitai and secured their written permission for an 'Indo-jin' named John to report on the day's purge to the English section of *Domei Tusin-sya*. Four outsize Domei crests were fixed to the car: Front, back, and sides. Before we left the office I had gathered from talking to Chinese staff in my office the antecedents to the tragedy I was soon to witness in the heart of Penang, in Georgetown to be exact.

As troops converged on Georgetown, huge searchlight

beams (maybe Verey lights left by the British) stabbed the night sky. Few at the time noticed the operation, but at the stroke of midnight a dozen soldiers assembled at the head of every street. They knocked, not gently but with all their might, at the door of house after house in the entire Georgetown area. Their quarry was mainly Chinese, but every home was searched and every head closely scrutinised, leaving most Malays, Indians and Eurasians well alone. It went like this:

Startled by the unusual bang, the inmates of a house sought refuge in their backyard, only to dash back into the house on hearing Nippon-go and seeing flashes of torchlight right in their privy. In the meantime, one of the men would open what remained of the door. If the poor fellow didn't know the martial law of surrendering by putting his hands up, he would get a quick clout. He was ordered out into the street in whatever he was wearing or not wearing at the time, followed by the entire household. Then the house was thoroughly searched and the front door sealed. And soldiers were detailed to guard the houses, both front and rear, until the erstwhile occupants returned, if at all.

Penang was at the time passing through a very hot spell, and most men, women and children were scantily clothed, if at all. The children more than filled the breaches; they clambered up the bodies of their mothers or sisters in such profusion as to cover the nudity. And the crowd had to stay on the roadside until the entire street was 'disinfected', as the Japanese would say. At seven in the morning, the pitiful crowd was ordered to move along the Market Square where by eight nearly six thousand had gathered from all parts of the town.

A commando, who was staying in Penang at the time as Nagai's guest, drove the Domei car and acted as my protector as the car came under the scrutiny of the Kempeitai. Most of the troops left us well alone on seeing the Domei crest but two or three stopped the car, and examined me *in toto*. They let go our car on being satisfied that I was as harmless as Gandhiji. Though I took particular care not to make it known to my interrogators that I was sadly deficient in Nippon-go, I fumbled once or twice when off-beat questions were put to me. Having somehow survived, our car was allowed to proceed to an alley by the beach, the alley that came to be known as Blood Alley among the Chinese.

As the car swerved in, I noted the extreme precautions the Kempeitai was taking to make the purge absolutely invisible to any but those authorised to be present. Shortly after our arrival, two lorry-loads of Malayan detectives, hand-picked by army secret service men, were unloaded in the alley. Each was covered from head to foot by a dark hood with narrow slits for eyes. Thirty of them covered one side of the alley sieve while another 30 took their position on the opposite side. About six feet separated them, thus about two hundred feet came within their close range, or either side of the road. They had long poles. As they took up their positions, the crowd which had been in the streets for more than eight hours began to wend its way to the examination point.

The procession – more a funeral procession – was the most pitiful I have ever seen. A hungry baby clutched at its mother's bosom and began to weep when it found its goal obstructed by the lean limbs of an elder brother on the mother's shoulders. Without lifting her head she gave the baby a pinch, and from then on the unearthly silence was not broken. Dutifully hungry, the baby was mum thereafter. Slowly, inexorably, the column of terrified people meandered to their doom. I noticed there were roughly seven hundred rows, each of six persons, most of the women smothered by half-a-dozen children. Behind the column of detectives was a row of soldiers keeping watch on neighbouring houses. The area appeared to be a cul-de-sac sealed off on all sides by soldiers at combat readiness.

As row upon row passed between the two columns of detectives, eagle eyes scrutinised them, and every now and then a hooded man would point his pole, and soldiers armed to the teeth waded in and removed a row or two from the passing parade. They were suspected Communists or their sympathisers, and they had been fingered. 'Operation Red Nettle' was over by eleven. Nearly four hundred men with some women and children were packed into seven military trucks and taken away from Blood Alley. The rest went home, presumably, and all was quiet.

I heard innumerable stories about what happened to the seven lorry-loads. Some said they were roasted alive; others contended that they were cast away in the wilderness of Borneo or the Celebes. The most plausible story I heard was this: They were taken to the beach, five miles from Bloody Alley, and each asked to dig a grave and stand in it. Then the Samurai leapt into the scene with his traditional sword. And each, or whatever remained of oneself, slumped into the self-made graves. They were swiftly covered with sand, swords cleaned, and curtain dropped. The Japanese eventually paid a stunning penalty for the purges they staged in Malaya and other countries they occupied. Thirty months after Blood Alley, Hiroshima and Nagasaki almost settled the blood debt.

On returning to the office about noon, Nagai asked me if I had seen 'everything'. I thought of replying 'Not quite', but breezily responded: 'Yes, I had a grandstand view, but doubted if my heart could stand the shock of the disembowelling.'

Feeling I was a bit taken aback by the day's events, Nagai gave me a little background to the story. From the notes I have been keeping with me for the past twenty-three years, I give a short summary of his talk in March 1943:

'Well, John, what you saw today might shake your confidence in us. You might wonder whether we are Buddhists at all. Your mind would naturally be vacillating – are we gentle and compassionate as we are known to be, or are we an arrogant, jealous and blood-thirsty people? You know, John-san, I love you as my own brother. We wouldn't slaughter innocent human beings unless their guilt has been proved.

'You know, we had been fighting in China for years before Pearl Harbour. By far the most productive region of China is Manchukuo which has been in our hands since 1930. Prince Pu-yi, whom Chiang Kai-shek and his Anglo–American collaborators branded as a Japanese puppet, is still nominally the ruler of the entire Manchukuo although for reasons of health he still occupies a palace miles from Mukden. He is the last surviving link of the old Manchu Dynasty.

'When we politely showed the Chinese the new Manchukuo's skyrocketing production figures and suggested China, too, could follow the lead, the old China Dragon hissed back at us and asked us to leave the mainland well alone. We merely tried to teach them the elements of modern economy.

'There is a mistaken notion abroad that we are, or rather were, at war with China. We are not. China is merely an incident. We told the powers-that-be in Nanking how Asia can reassert itself and remain as a separate entity absolutely independent of Anglo–American aid. They wouldn't listen to us. So, the younger brother was constrained to flog the elder until he learned modern economics which is far removed from the teachings of Kung Fu-tse.[1] We've given the Dragon a respite until we finish off the Anglo–Americans.

'Chinese overseas are little different from Chinese on the mainland. Those who resist us in China are indeed Communists, and there are spies around you who will be carrying tales to Chiang Kai-shek. We knew from the underground a good number of Communist spies would be contacting rich people in Penang yesterday. So, the round-up was not the result of a mad hunt but a deliberate bombing of their hide-outs at a time when they were filled to capacity.'

I kept absolutely silent and Nagai began to suspect that he had failed to convince me. Was this fellow still on the 'other side?'

---

[1] Confucius.

He continued: 'Like you we, too, are oppressed to see women and children being slashed to death like chicken. We've caught not only in Singapore but in Rangoon, Jakarta, Manila and Hong Kong a filthy Chinese woman roaming the streets for alms with a cartload of babies on and about her whose main occupation is to pass a note from a Communist leader to a prominent man in the area in which she would apparently be begging. We have evidence before us that some of the women we have liquidated had been carrying fiats from the Communists to well-to-do Chinese demanding money, arms and ammunition. Here in this country, too, the same devious game was afoot. There are thousands of Chinese who fled into the jungles to menace our rear whenever our army is on the move. You know they are fed by people whom you and I know as docile subjects of Nippon. If and when such people are caught, don't you think we have to burn them alive? If you want India to be free we have to burn the nettles first.'

I kept nodding my head. Did they burn the five hundred that morning? Perhaps he wanted me to rise and shout 'Banzai' to Emperor Hirohito and reaffirm my steadfast loyalty. I said they could have been shot instead, that is, if their guilt had been proved beyond any doubt. Nagai sharply butted in and remarked rather cynically that gunpowder might be very cheap in my country, not in his. He said the Japanese would use a gun and waste gunpowder only when absolutely necessary. Those whom I saw in the alley round-up, he said with unusual vehemence, were the scum of the earth fit to be burned alive or cut up and thrown to vultures. Nippon had far more important use for modern weapons. Blood rushed into his jugular veins and his neck swelled up. He rose from his seat, shaking with emotion, and with upraised arms murmured something about *Tenno-Heika* (Emperor Hirohito). And as he inclined toward me, for the first time a streak of terror passed through me. Was he trying to do me in? He leaned forward and dipped into my breast pocket. He fished out a packet of cigarettes, and we chain-smoked until the Chinese boy called us in to lunch. By and by the day's events were forgotten. And, with as much skill as we could muster, Jose and I fulfilled our daily assignments with apparent devotion.

In addition to writing the daily broadcast, beamed at India, I had to okay every 'subbed' cable before it was distributed. And as days went by it seemed to me I could get away without impairing the efficiency of the locally-recruited staff. The time for Bose's arrival in Shonan was approaching, Nagai was pestered with letters from Shonan Domei asking him to expedite my return. As we sat down to dinner one evening, Nagai asked me to get ready to return to Shonan as soon as possible. Hitherto, I could neither visit the summit of Penang Hill (from which I was told I could see the tail of India being twisted by Britain for more and more farm output to feed her vast armies) nor the idyllic botanic gardens. And I decided to ask Nagai for two days' leave before going back to Shonan.

Then I noticed that our *amah* herself came to our table with a tray of mashed potatoes garnished with greens. On seeing her, I recalled her strange intuition the day before the purge which drove her to town to collect eleven more to her already bloated brood.

How she smelled danger twenty-four hours in advance remained a mystery to me until a friend told me of her association with a highly-placed Japanese officer. She had under her protection teenaged girls whom she presented to a chosen few for the duration. The instinct for self-preservation! She was known to be the fifth wife of a Chinese millionaire who was then safe abroad.

13

On The Hill

EVER SINCE I joined Domei in April 1942, I hadn't had a single holiday because I well knew the Japanese frowned on holidays as long as their enemy managed to show themselves up at least-expected points on the periphery of their erstwhile empire stretching from the Indian Ocean to the Pacific. The Allies were hurting from Dunkirk[1] and, in the Axis view, a few more days of bombing would wreck the entire British Isles. And until the surrender of Anglo–Americans, who could afford to have a holiday? On Nagai assuring me that he would hold the fort for three days, I had the temerity to sneak out of the office on a sight-seeing tour.

With a local-born Indian man who spoke Hokkien[2] as well as Malay I proceeded by car early one morning to the foot of Penang Hill, from where a miniature railway went up the 2,700ft hill. My companion, Raju, was a casual acquaintance of mine in Singapore. A few days before the Japanese stormed into Penang,

---

1 Pullout of defeated Allied troops on the European mainland.
2 South China dialect.

Raju had managed to squeeze his wife and two children into a cargo boat bound for Madras. Roughly forty, he was raving mad to ascertain some news about his family in India. His wife and two sons, if lucky, might have reached their destination. Raju was sure they would be properly looked after if they contacted his distant cousin in Madras. But if the woman, practically a stranger to India, failed to contact his relative? On his bursting into tears, I told him there was a way out. What it was I couldn't tell him then. I hinted that the Japanese might move across north-west Burma with an Indian army recruited locally. Raju reclined his head on my lap, and implored me to do whatever I could to have him enlisted in that army when the time came. I replied I would do my best for him. And the car soon came to a halt at the foot of the hill railway. After telling the driver to return to the station around four in the evening, we bought our tickets and boarded a rear wagon which had fewer soldiers than the two in front. The few who were in our wagon appeared to be in unusually high spirits. After perusing my identity card they got very chummy with me. Despite the linguistic barrier, I talked to them in broken Nippon-go embellished here and there by Malay or English words. Nothing of past or present campaigns. Like embarrassed people everywhere, we talked of the weather. Few who loved their lives exceeded the weather barrier! What we talked mattered little but how we made ourselves understood was indeed fascinating. Left severely to himself, a Japanese man is probably the most harmless person in the world. But two or more in a bunch, on level terms, are absolutely irrepressible. I smiled and they too smiled in return, as the wee train screeched to a stop at the top station. They went their way, and we ours.

I soon presented myself before the Japanese manager of a resthouse. On the strength of my identity papers, he agreed to give us luncheon in the afternoon for one military dollar per head. (At the time *kopi-o* and noodle soup in town cost no less than twenty-five dollars!) Domei papers did the trick. We leisurely meandered through the winding hill paths dotted by elegant cottages and mansions, almost hidden from the plain below. Temperature here at noon was similar to what it was on the shore at six in the morning. While stepping off the train in the morning I felt it was rather unwise not to have worn a warm jacket or at least a muffler around my neck. Anyway, the stroll was most bracing.

It was an old preserve of the British civil servants. English-type cottages nestled on the hillside with beautiful gardens of outsize roses and cannas growing on earth carved out from the hillside. Nearly every one of the cottages, now reserved for army bosses, was under the supervision of a Chinese servant and his *amah*-wife. The largesse from the cottages helped keep alive thousands of Chinese in the town below. It was said the food was sent 'by the tube'. I still wonder how they got past four sentry posts on the way down.

Later, we went to Domei's hill bungalow where the *amah* welcomed us with a pot of steaming green tea. It was champagne to Raju, a tea addict, who had scarcely tasted tea since surrender. Living in Domei hostelry, I sipped green tea every morning and evening. But the large mass of civilians were at the time learning to erase from their memory the taste of coffee and tea. People were concentrating on finding more substantial food. There never was any threat of famine in Malaya, thanks to Thai and Indo-Chinese farmers and enterprising Chinese small-boat operators who managed to feed those not blessed with Japanese rations. No country would have done better than Malaya in the last war, thanks to Chinese perseverance.

We soon returned to the resthouse for lunch, which was as wholesome as any you could get in a Chinese hotel before the war. *Meehoon,* or noodle soup, fried fish and green tea for just one (military) dollar! Japanese wages looked poor but would go a long way if you knew how and where to spend them. In the backyard Raju heard some muffled Chinese voices. As a butterfly to a rose, he was lured to a mahjong game. Good riddance! It took him nearly three hours to lose his four dollars. Meanwhile I rested under a spreading bougainvillea in the adjoining park. I gazed eagerly westward at the Bay of Bengal, blinked and blinked at nothingness until I fell fast asleep.

Did I, or did I not, see in my reverie a bullock in the west, yes, a famished Indian bullock, whose tail was time and again twisted or squeezed until it yielded larger and larger volumes of war material? Ah, the Bengal famine was much worse than what we feared at the time. Hadn't we to fly post-haste to Delhi to give first aid to the starving bullock? Was not my family beckoning me from India? If I hadn't been roused from my reverie by Raju, I fear I would have somnambulated myself downhill, westward, Indiaward, to nothingness.

Poor Raju was a deflated balloon. He looked daggers at the Chinese boy, his opponent, whom he swore to flatten whenever he could afford to come up the hill with a lunch basket and a moderate purse. In the name of all the gods and goddesses in the Hindu pantheon, he swore he would get his own back some day. His heat was a bit subsided by the time I fully returned from dreamland. We hurried to the top station, and round about five we reached the bottom where the Domei car awaited my return.

'I hope we could meet somewhere under different circumstances,' Raju said as he took leave of me. Six months later, he joined the Indian National Army and moved out to Burma. A true son of India, I do not know what happened to him.

Early the following morning, armed with a lunch basket (I had to borrow from the 'summit' a thermos flask), I was taken to the botanic gardens in the office car about eight in the morning. As I got out at the entrance to the garden Indian workmen crowded round me with a hundred questions. One young fellow named Das was eager to know whether he could go to India that year (1943), or at the latest the next. His uncle had been to Madura before the war and had found a match for him, and the wedding would have taken place the previous year but for the war. Her name, he whispered in my ears, was Lakshmi. This blasted war, thought I, had ruined many a country but had also squeezed millions upon millions of innocent lives. Like Raju (and myself) poor Das was searching in the darkness for some road to light his way – to India. Without mentioning Bose by name, I hinted that many an unexpected event might ginger us up in 1943. Soon Das was pacified and he accompanied me in my stroll through the gardens.

The gardens had not suffered much by comparative neglect since British departure. The hedges were neatly trimmed to geometrical designs but the swards cried out for mowing. Most types of tropical trees and shrubbery, ranging from Burma teak to Casesalpinia indicia and flamboyant Hibiscus rosasinensis, could be seen at their best. The flame-of-the-forest was truly ablaze, and the garden on the whole appeared to be the best I had seen outside India.

Cases of fruit collected from the gardens – pineapples, durian and rambutans, passion-fruit, etc. – were daily dispatched by rail to army, navy, and air force HQs in Shonan and elsewhere. Malaya is a rich treasure house of exotic fruit most of which were anathema to the Japanese. As I have said previously, they would not touch the mango unless fortified by sanitary precautions. Like most non-Malayans, Japanese wouldn't dare touch durian (botanically akin to the Indian jackfruit). Like rum, tobacco and opium, once you stomach durian it would continue to enchant you to the end of your days.

For two hours I sat on the grass in the enchanting paradise, thinking of possible ways of escape to Bharat Mata, my mother-country. In reality, there was hardly any loophole for escape. I couldn't, then, even think of a possible Japanese surrender, though enough indications were available of a future counter-attack by the Americans who had, by then, begun the preliminaries to island-hopping. Anyhow, I made one solid decision that day, and that was to remain as far away from Shonan as possible without arousing any suspicion.

I got so ravenously hungry that I quickly demolished what was contained in my lunch basket capped with a cup of green tea. Refreshed, I wandered through the gardens. Like the British prisoners of war at the time, their gardens, too, were vegetating.

Few in Malaya at the time dreamt that the Americans and the British were finalising the strategic details of the Normandy landings simultaneously with crippling blows on the Japanese navy, which was already having difficulties in keeping open supply lines to their far-flung troops from Pacific islands to north Burma. Those Japanese difficulties were not known to the masses in Malaya, thanks to Kempeitai and Domei. But I knew very well that things were not going as well as the Japanese would like them to be. So, the sooner Jose and I got out of Shonan the better for us. With this decision uppermost in my mind, I sauntered to the gate to await the car when Das, who had been in urgent consultation with his comrades, came to tell me they were ready to join up 'if there was any way'. I told him that I, too, was anxious to enlist in an Indian army and would attempt to open the door to India which was presently barred. As my car stopped at the gate I said goodbye to Das and departed quickly. We were in the same boat as Netaji.

After a hurried meal at the office mess I hastily packed my bag, and Nagai and I drove to the jetty where we had to wait for ten minutes before the ferry to the mainland arrived. Nagai told me confidentially that he himself might have to leave for Leyte in the Philippines very shortly and he would certainly say '*Sayonara*' (goodbye) to me in Shonan before leaving.

I was agreeably surprised to be ushered into a well-upholstered first-class compartment as I presented my ticket (with a chit from Domei) at the station. In Malaya both before and after the war a first-class ticket means a bed for oneself, with pushbutton near your cushions to summon an orderly, if needed. In India where the first rail track was laid more than a hundred years ago a rail journey means survival of the fittest. You will need to be lucky to survive by the time you reached your destination. We had crossed over into northern Selangor by the time I got up late the following morning. Most occupants of nearby couches went on sleeping until the train touched Kuala Lumpur. It took a further fifteen hours to reach Shonan where a Domei car awaited me. I was amazed. Why were Indians being treated so well? First-class travel and a waiting car? Ah, there was something up the Japanese sleeves.

That Bose was ordered out to the Far East had been known to every Japanese employee of Domei but the news was not allowed to be leaked out. Although I appeared to be Domei's trusted Indian newsman, I did not officially know of it until a few more weeks slipped by, though I had heard from one source that Bose had escaped from Calcutta and was known to be either in Rome or Berlin.

Domei's Greater East Asia expert, Inoue Suzuki, summoned me for secret talks as soon as I called at the office on my return from Penang. He praised me for having helped put up a new rung in Domei's ladder. The conversation went something like this:

'Ah, how's Penang, John-san?'

'A microcosm of Asia on the plains below with Kashmir superimposed on the Hill. Hard to find the like of it!'

'You should've seen your fatherland from the top of the Hill!'

'Oh, my mother country, you mean. Her eyes are sunken, cheeks hollow. Lean, almost emaciated, and hungry ...'

'I see your broadcasts to Delhi are well received in quarters for whom they're intended.'

I blinked, and he continued: 'Well, we've to ginger them up a bit. Make 'em more and more stinging.'

'I would do my best for my country.'

'Instead of the 500 words as at present, double them for India from tomorrow ... I'm frightfully busy, John-san.'

Most unusually, quite a number of small fry fawned upon me with toothy smiles, offered me cigarettes, and ordered green tea. They hovered about my desk and their faces beamed not with laughter but with gratitude. I kept wondering what it was all bout until one told me a popular Japanese magazine commended me for 'the sock in the jaw administered daily to Anglo–Americans'. Though my name was not divulged, most Japanese in Domei knew to whom the reference alluded. Old Delhi pointed an accusing finger at me, and Tokyo commended me! I wondered where all this was going to end up.

Returning to my flat in the evening, I met some of my old friends with whom I had had a frank discussion relating to Indians' future course of action. Though not yet officially confirmed, it was known to every Indian in Malaya at the time that Bose was shortly to appear in Shonan. The consensus of opinion then was to join the INA (Indian National Army) and proceed to Burma in the first instance, no matter what happens. Whether the decision was born out of real loyalty to India, or out of sheer necessity to escape the growing distress of occupation was, and still is, a moot point. However, INA was never short of manpower; we all hoped that superior Japanese strategy would come into play. Undoubtedly the Japanese were sincere in preparing the groundwork for the thrust into India via Imphal, but their naval strength at the time was being fast whittled down in the Coral Sea, Midway, Guadalcanal and elsewhere in the Pacific. This was the reason why Japan could not help the INA to the extent she desired. Well, we all agreed at the time the best we could do in the circumstances was to move nearer and nearer India, whatever the price we might have to pay.

Krishna, my cook, asked me for the umpteenth time, 'When can we get back home?' I told him what I knew and reminded him of an old Indian proverb that admonished: 'Can't you wait for the steam to pass since you have waited so long to bake the pudding?' Wait until our redeemer arrived, and everything would be all right. Pacified, Krishna retired to bed. About ten, I too went to bed but I couldn't sleep. I kept rolling in bed for about an hour when a voice was heard in the staircase. Then there was a loud knock on the front door. I opened the door, and a drunken Japanese officer with this inseparable sword, revolver, etc., sauntered in. His slit-eyes had narrowed to a thread under *samsu*, *sake*, or whatever it was that filled him to capacity. He smelt short of hell – with a distant stink of the latrine.

He harangued me in Nippon-go and my sketchy, noncommittal, monosyllabic replies made him only more irascible. He found out I had not picked up Nippon-go as fluently as I should have. Fingering his revolver menacingly, he asked me if I was hiding a girl in my flat. Emphatically, I replied 'No'. He searched the house – and being the second search in thirteen months, Krishna appeared to be practically at ease. So was I. As he reclined on my sofa, he kept moaning, 'Where's the rady?' I said I hadn't the least idea. As the clock struck twelve, my uninvited guest felt visibly moved, and fumbled door ward as if to get away. But he again slumped on the sofa, an incoherent, immovable mass of tipsy human material.

He told me his name was something akin to Muragama, though he himself had pronounced it tipsily as 'Mulagutawney[3].' Roughly 35, Muragama came for dinner to a Eurasian home on the first floor, accompanied by five others. Their hosts were the Lynds, our neighbours. Geoffrey was an electrician and his wife a teacher. Ever since Muragama found out that the Lynds had two comely daughters, always behind doors whenever alien visitors knocked at their door, he came in more and more frequently and at unearthly times with whatever he could steal from army food dumps. The previous evening there was a *makan besar* (gala dinner) at the Lynds with liberal supplies of *samsu*. At eight when

---

3 An in-joke. The word means pepper water. The l would have come out as r.

the dinner was over, Muragama was anxious to present 'his' girl to the comrades. It was then that Geoffrey told him the girl had gone to his sister's and would be back only on the morrow. Because they had to be back in their barracks before nine at the latest, his friends soon left. Even at the peril of a court martial, Muragama was determined to make a night hunt for the girl that he lusted after. That was how he came to my flat. I would have found it hard to escape a court martial myself if the military police had visited my home at the time Muragama was lying drunk on my sofa. By one it appeared that Muragama was fast asleep, and I switched off the lights and went back to bed.

I got up about five in the morning, and woke up the intruder. He seemed to be in a frenzy as soon as he opened his eyes. His guilt writ in his face, he fled. Middle Road never saw him again.

The days dragged on until June when it was known that Bose would shortly land in Shonan. The news electrified the entire Indian community in Malaya. From tapper to barrister, almost every Indian eagerly looked forward to the day of his idol's arrival.

As for myself, I had almost forgotten the need to feign illness and recuperate in the Cameron Highlands, miles from danger. I told an office friend that I would join up with the first Indian battalion organised under Japanese direction. Eventually I heard that the Japanese would not release me from Domei. I was again in a flux. Where was Destiny leading me?

14

'Challo Dilli!'

IN THE SECOND week of June 1943 a brief note appeared in the *Azad Hind* saying that Bose, who had presided over the Tripura session of the Indian National Congress in 1938, would shortly arrive in Shonan to lead an army of Indians, men as well as women, to their motherland. A week later another note said that the Netaji had indeed arrived from Germany and that he would be addressing a gathering of Indian PoWs on the Padang that evening. To Indians in Malaya and Singapore, roughly 500,000 souls, this was staggering news – we were no longer destined to wander in the wilderness. We had a definite object to live for – 'Challo Dilli!'

No sooner had the Netaji stepped out of a limousine on the Padang than a hefty *jawan* (Indian soldier), shaking all over with intense excitement, yelled 'Netaji-*ki-jai*!' (victory to Netaji). Nobody who took part in the meeting can, to this day, offer a plausible explanation for all that happened there in the next twenty minutes. There was feverish yelling of nationalist slogans for almost fifteen minutes. Oh, what a ballyhoo!

As *jawans* danced in pairs under the refrain of '*Jai!*' thousands of civilians in the periphery shouted themselves hoarse. What a babel of languages: Tamil, Malayalam, Kannada, Telugu, Hindi, Bengali, etc! And superimposed on all this was a hissing staccato from the dais, '*Banzai!*' When it all died down, the Netaji addressed us in English (what an irony!), then he switched to Hindi. (If ever, almost 500 million Indians, have to continue as a democratic nation we must cling to English. Take it or leave it.)

For the Indians locked up in the Light of the South, what mattered much more than the Netaji's speech that day was the fact that he was *with* us. We of the Press sat right before the rostrum, representatives of Domei, the Shonan *Shimbun* (a faint image of the old, British-owned *Straits Times*) and *Azad Hind*. Netaji told us of his plan to organise an Indian National Army (INA) with our final goal New Delhi, 'now bursting with British'. He wondered whether guns would be needed at all to take us to the capital. If SEAC tried to stop the INA they would be caught up by Indians in the rear (unarmed) and Indians in front. Exciting prospects! Though with difficulty, we all learned to chant our famed national songs such as *Jana Gana Mana* and *Vande Mataram*. After his speech, the Netaji was somehow extricated from the melee, and his aides smuggled him out to the car. Thousands of PoWs followed the car, singing, dancing and feinting *ju-jitsu* moves, newly taught by the Japanese. Never have I seen such uncontrolled mass hysteria.

My biggest surprise was yet to come. A week later, a meeting of Indian women was convened at the old Anzac club in Singapore, now converted into an INA annexe. The president was Dr Lakshmi Swaminathen, and the speaker Bose. Roughly six hundred Indian women assembled there of whom five hundred joined the new women's wing of the INA, called the Rani[1] of Jhansi Regiment with Dr (then Colonel) Lakshmi as overall commander. Her mother was the distinguished Indian parliamentarian, Mrs Ammu Swaminathen (née Nair), and her father, the late Dr Swaminathen of Madras. All that is best in Kerala's Malayalees and Tamils of Madras is blended harmoniously in Dr Lakshmi's delicate face. She typifies Indian womanhood. Soon after her graduation from the Madras Medical College, she married Captain Hanumanthayya, a pilot from Mysore. Somehow she wriggled out of wedlock, and in 1940 set up private practice in Singapore. And that was how she was picked up by the Netaji to lead INA's women. During or after the war she married Lieut-Col Sehgal, and settled down in Uttar Pradesh.

I knew her from 1940 when she came to Singapore. I knew from my own experience how she gave vial after vial of drugs to needy men and women who flocked to her nursing home in Katong. After being hard at work in her dispensary from morn till eve she would go out in the evenings visiting people who needed help. Then came the call to arms, and she set out to make a fighting regiment out of the thousands of stay-at-home Indian women in Malaya. Judged by modern military standards, the Rani of Jhansi Regiment proved nought in the battle-fields. I am not very certain

---

1 Queen.

if the 'Ranis' were ever called upon to fight with the frontline troops but to see the women march through the streets, guns to the fore, was terrific. Was it possible for any man to stay behind? We were all itching to go to Burma but in my case the Domei was unwilling to release me. So Jose and I were left behind in Shonan.

The metamorphosis that occurs when people are called upon to fight for one's own country is an uplifting sight. India, under the British, was just a congeries of hundreds or even thousands of intramural allegiances or, to put it more liberally, introvert loyalties, so much so that a Sikh from Punjab in the north had little sense of brotherliness with a Tamil from the south – ideal for the imposition of foreign domination. This communal situation had appeared to serve the interests of the ruler and the ruled for nearly a century and a half. In the circumstances, Indians in Shonan in mid-1943 felt we were at the bedside of Mother India in her birth pangs to bring forth the new India. All of us had been uprooted from our normal way of life and were waiting for a leader to guide us back to our country. India should be free when we reached her borders, otherwise we would have Japanese arms to defeat the British. We conjured up phantoms that would take us home on fleets of magic carpets. The British would simply flee. Indian and Japanese imagination created all manner of marvellous scenarios. A mere spark from the INA was all that was required to inflame the entire Indian subcontinent. That spark never made contact with the mass of the people, but it was clear that the game was up for the British Raj. The birth of the INA was enough to suggest that India was in the kind of ferment that Russia was in 1917 or Paris on the eve of the storming of the Bastille in the French of Revolution. Even Churchill could not stem the inexorable march of events. Two years after Japan surrendered, Lord Mountbatten, who led SEAC during the war, stepped down from the *gadi*[2] as Britain's last Viceroy, granting India full independence.

This was only a glint in the eye of Indians in Shonan when Netaji arrived in 1943. Thousands of Indians applied to enlist in the INA and besieged the INA office all day. Practically every able-bodied man was immediately drafted in. After they were taught to shoot, and shoot to kill, the recruits were sent to Rangoon, regiment by regiment. The men's enlistment, training and arming were under the direct supervision of the Netaji, and the women's under Colonel Lakshmi, who was herself rather new to holding a gun, let alone firing it. However, after a few hours on the shooting range she was reasonably good at it. Her silk sari gave way to an officer's khaki uniform. Within a month almost five hundred women had rushed to the colours. Among them were rubber tappers and gardeners as well as middle-class housewives, teachers, typists, nurses and professionals. Girls from sweet 17 to matrons of 40 or more enlisted in the Rani of Jhansi Regiment. What impelled them to enlist?

Indian women of early Shonan were mostly of a home-bound type and, like women of captive populations everywhere, they

---

2 Horse-drawn state coach.

dreaded Japanese soldiers.[3] Drunk with power and victory over the 'foreign devils', Japanese soldiers often ran amok in kampongs far from the sight of their superior officers. They were known to have raped and plundered throughout the countryside. The very sight of a woman would inflame them, so women stayed out of sight. It was hinted in Indian quarters that most women recruits were enlisting out of fear of the Japanese ruffians. Khaki was an effective defence. 'Challo Dilli!' was even more powerful. Whatever the reason, patriotism or fear of Japanese atrocity, there was a terrific rush of recruits to the Ranis. Every Saturday afternoon batches of Ranis could be seen moving through the streets with military precision. Until the previous day the deadliest weapon they had touched was the kitchen knife. But in August 1943 they had a world of confidence with guns to nurse.

I have often wondered what impact the INA would have made if the push into Imphal was made in the middle of 1942 instead of in the last quarter of 1943. The Bengal famine was at its worst in mid-1942 and the Calcutta Corporation was moving thousands of famished corpses to the burning ghats every day. By the time of the Imphal attack by INA troops Britain had overcome the worst setbacks of the war and was better prepared. Much water had flown down the Ganges in the crucial fifteen months.

---

[3] The Japanese Imperial Army enslaved between 80,000 and 200,000 women and girls from 1932 until the end of the war in 1945. Most were brought from Korea, with many also from China, Japan, the Dutch East Indies and PoW camps . They were known as comfort women and sent to comfort stations throughout the occupied territories to serve Japanese soldiers. It was a well-kept secret that was exposed after the war.

It was an open secret in India that Nehru and Bose did not see eye to eye on the conduct of Indian National Congress affairs. Bose's extremist views were anathema to Nehru and his staunch supporter, the popular Mohandas Gandhi, who was propagating non-violence and civil disobedience as political weapons. That was probably the Indian Government did not do quite as much as it should have to rehabilitate those brave men and women.

Nehru, until his death, maintained a sort of *non possumus*[4] attitude to everything connected with the INA, that is, Bose. If the INA had succeeded in Imphal millions would have assembled at the border and carried Bose on their shoulders to Calcutta, and thence to Delhi. And Nehru would have been India's No. 2. Whatever the might-have-been, one cannot help feeling that the Nehru-Bose feud harmed the interests of the men and women who had the guts to open fire on the British. Some paid the supreme price. So I say, better late than never. Give the devil his due. The INA should have a monument in Delhi. And let India's younger generation grow up to salute the INA on January 23, birthday of the Netaji. It is downright foolish to forget our past.

---

4 Not possible, cannot do.

15

The World War

THERE IS STILL a great deal of controversy in India on the life and work of Subhas Chandra Bose and the ill-fated INA. It is mainly attributable to the deft propaganda carried out by the British in the closing stage of their 'Indian Empire'. Most Indians outside West Bengal, the home state of the Netaji, seemed to have been taken in by this. Until the war's end, or, to be precise, until India became independent in 1947, my countrymen on the whole viewed Bose and his so-called masters, Nazi Germany and Japan, with extreme aversion. I can well understand why it should have been so at the time. It was precisely to create such an impression that Britain maintained highly paid publicity officers with SEAC in Calcutta. But I fail to understand why the effect of such vindictive and negative propaganda is still felt in most Indian states outside West Bengal. Highly placed Indians in free India dismiss Bose as a heady adventurer whose military mission did little to persuade Britain to give India her freedom. That was exactly what the British wanted Indians to believe. But the old is gradually giving way to the new, and the rising India has generally come to realise that the saint Gandhiji, moderate Nehru and extremist Bose all combined to force the British to abandon India to her own devices.

When Bose vanished after the Japanese surrender, it was reported that his plane had crashed in Taipeh, Formosa (Taiwan) and Bose was said to have died in a nearby hospital. After cremation his ashes were placed in an urn and installed in a Buddhist temple in Tokyo. So goes the Japanese story that was later verified by Capt Shah Nawaz Khan[1] whom the Government of India sent to Formosa and Japan to make enquiries. But many in India feel that the last phase of Bose's life is still shrouded in mystery. The plane crash was said to have occurred more than a week after Japan surrendered to General MacArthur in August 1945. Most of the important airfields in Japan were under American control. From what little I know of the Japanese mind, I do not think that a plane would be sent from Saigon, which was still under Japanese control, all the way to Tokyo to deliver the Netaji into the hands of the US military administration. Absolutely not. I cannot believe the Bose chapter ended in Taipeh. I and many others cling to the view that he may be meditating in the Himalayas!

I hadn't had much to do with Bose in Singapore, beyond interviewing him three times on behalf of Domei. The weight of history sat heavily on his shoulders. He had a grave, morose expression on his face. Few saw him smile during his brief sojourn in Malaya. I remember listening to him addressing the Rani Ki

---

[1] He was an Indian Army Captain, taken prisoner by Japanese in Singapore, joined the INA, captured by British troops in Burma, tried and sentenced to death in India for waging war on the Crown, but released following widespread protests.

Jhansi Regiment on the Padang in Singapore in June 1943. He recounted the Rani's gallant fight to the end against very heavy odds. As he paused a moment to survey the mass of women before him, their faces glowing in the emotion that he was creating with his words, Bose was visibly moved and covered his face with a handkerchief. As his words spread like honey on the mass of heaving women, as he exhorted them in the name of a brave Rani, the uniformed ranks rose as one to cry ' Challo Dilli!' Whatever the INA's failings in the theatre of operations on the Indo-Burma border, to his millions of admirers in India Bose lives not only today but for an infinite space of time.

To be frank, not until I saw the women's demonstration at the old ANZAC club in Singapore in 1943 did I realise what a rare honour it was mine to be counted an Indian, one with the Rajahs and Ranis who were then shortly to go to war for my country's freedom. And I did my part at the editorial desk. With my daily broadcasts beamed at Delhi, I imagined myself to be personally at war with the British months before the INA reached India's borders. What made me breathe fire and brimstone at the British at the time? I can honestly say the British with whom, or under whom, I had had to work both in India and Singapore had been scrupulously just in their dealings with me, though the average Indian knew that his country had been nearly bled white by a century and half of British overlordship. 'Give us back at least the carcass of India before you are forced to leave,' I used to howl day in and day out from Singapore. Not because I hated the British but because I loved India more. A British security officer detailed to examine me after the war summarily dismissed my case on hearing that statement. If Nazi Germany or Fascist Italy had ever caught a newsman in my plight he would have been summarily shot. It is instances like these that have endeared us to the British which helped them hold sway over us for over 150 years. Thanks to the British, I am spared to write this book. If ever I am forced to have another overlord I would run post-haste to London.

On the day the Netaji made his first speech in Shonan, the Domei broadcast this appeal from Shonan Radio to 'our poor hungry brethren in British India':

'We extremely sympathise with you in your present unenviable plight. Because the British have taken away all your food to batten their armies, you may be in grave peril.

'Many thousands had already fallen in the streets of Calcutta due to sheer starvation and many more would follow them to the graveyard if bags of rice presently rotting in barns stretching from Mandalay, a few hundred miles off Calcutta, to Manila in the Philippines are not forthwith rushed to you. But the Tommy eats the food God has given you. He's idly sucking at his lollipops, while more and more Krishnas and Sarasvatis with their little ones perish on your streets daily.

'God would not allow such a catastrophe to stalk the world indefinitely. The Almighty has a design to bring relief immediately to the poor and starving Indians. The Netaji who escaped from a British prison in Calcutta, has reached us in Shonan, via Berlin! Would listeners pass on this information to his near and dear ones at home? He is in first class health, bustling with energy. He would shortly arrive in Calcutta with lorryloads of Siam rice – sorry, it will take some more time to assemble wheat. How miraculous it is! Westward he first fled; from the east he would shortly call at your home with RICE and later WHEAT. India will have plenty soon if only the British would withdraw.

'Look out! Shri Bose, whom we call Netaji now, might return to his home any day now at the head of an Indian National Army (also with the Rani of Jhansi Regiment) if the British wouldn't walk out before he arrives. Unless we are forced to slaughter, we do want to return like satyagrahis. But if we are resisted ... woe unto the British. Tommies would be knocked out with their sweethearts, lollipops, and all.

'Listen to us everyday at 16:00 hrs GMT or 20:45 Calcutta time. follow our directions to wipe out poverty and the British from Indian soil. Allow them to return home bag and baggage unmolested. They wouldn't easily forget what befell them in Singapore early in 1942. Well, our time is up. Namashte!'.

Such verbal torpedoes were hurled at the British day in and day out from all the radio stations that fell to the Japanese in Southeast Asia in the early stage of the Pacific War. After the war a British official met me at my office. I told him all that had happened in Singapore during the British absence. I told him I did not hate the British; I only loved India more. I wasn't arrested; but was allowed to go scot-free, like the Indian PoW's caught on the borders of Manipur.

Twice I met the Netaji at Press interviews in Shonan. The first was a few days after his arrival in Shonan and the second weeks after the INA's first ceremonial parade on the Padang and its departure to Rangoon. The women's corps, the Rani Jhansi Regiment, was well covered by the INA throughout the journey to Rangoon, both in front and in the rear. We heard the Netaji was meeting the Press 'in connection with the INA's departure to the warfront'. But, as was to be expected, he actually met us two or three days after the army had reached Rangoon.

At the formal inauguration of the INA, there was a passing-out parade on the Padang. For the first time we saw an Indian army without British officers. No Rising Sun flag was seen anywhere except atop the municipal buildings. Column after column of Indian troops, men and women, smartly goose-stepped across the maidan, bowing to nothing but the Indian tricolour. Nearly four-fifths of the INA were ex-prisoners, the others being recruited locally. It seemed they lacked nothing in equipment. And all eyes were moist as they saluted the Indian tricolour, and then the Rising Sun. The youth I met at the botanical gardens in Penang, Das, was now an infantryman. I still wonder if he ever met his fiancée in Madura.

When I first met him in 1943, Bose appeared to be ten years younger than what he really was. He looked hardly thirty-seven when he was in fact 47. His general's uniform was topped by a green forage-cap cocked to one side which was reminiscent of a Gandhi-cap. Once the cap was removed, he looked slightly above his age, baldness having invaded either side of his head. I know from the 'inside' he well doubted from the outset if the Japanese could render as much help as the INA required. However, the dice was cast – there was no retreat.

Failure of the Imphal thrust sealed the fate of the INA. Whoever had not fallen in battle or were not taken prisoner hastily withdrew. How those men and women ultimately reached Singapore is an epic scarcely every publicised. Many fell on the way. Everybody, including the Netaji himself, had to footslog over impenetrable jungles separating Burma from Thailand. They had to evade frequent aerial bombardment as well to cross into Thailand.

Like the British, the Japanese must sink or swim with their navy. And by 1944, attrition of Japan's Navy had mounted to formidable proportions. It was more than halved by this time.

The Japanese were definitely on the defensive, and those not taken in by Axis propaganda knew that the end was within sight. To be frank, even the Japanese themselves, except those in the High Command, didn't quite know of the American ascendancy at the time. Placed as I was in what appeared as a top or semi-top position on Domei English section, I well knew the time was up to flee Shonan, the earlier the better. But circumstances, as they shaped later, completely befuddled my estimates at the time.

Japan had bitten off a far larger chunk than she could ever chew or digest. Her army was far too thinly scattered from Sumatra in the Indian Ocean to south and north Pacific. But the Navy's losses were more than made good by the growing number of Kamikaze ('divine wind') raids carried out under the direction of Admiral Takijiro Ohnishi[2]. And yet, by stages, Japan was

---

2 When Japan surrendered in August 1945, Ohnishi committed *harakiri* to atone for the thousands of lives he sent on *kamikaze* deaths.

inexorably moving toward abject surrender. But early in 1944 neither the U.S. nor Japan could foresee it.

I for one did not think that Britain would leave the entire Pacific strategy to United States. As I saw it then, Britain which was far out of the woods by early 1944 would have had to make a sally into the then East Indies to synchronise with Brigadier Orde Wingate's putsch into Burma as well as the progress of the U.S. island-hopping in the Pacific. But unfortunately this did not come about. She was far too preoccupied elsewhere. And Britain apparently lost face in the multiracial eyes of the Orient. Another Colonial Power, France, lost hers first in her capitulation to Nazi Germany in 1940 and once again at Dienbienphu, in Indo-China, in 1954. These are some of the reasons why Colonialism or as it is today called Neo-Colonialism is fast slipping out of favour in Asia and Africa. It is in this context that the historian will assuredly find a place for Netaji Subhas Chandra Bose whose last days are still shrouded in mystery.

Bose and Nehru, it may be recalled, had been in a neck-and-neck race for India's freedom, pursuing two different routes to the same goal. To put it mildly, there were serious political cleavages between the two. No wonder, Nehru's India, so busy preoccupied with laying the foundations of free India, discarded the INA with scant attention. I doubt if post-Nehru India would view INA in a perspective other than Nehru's. However I do hope future generations in India would see that the travails of those brave men and women of India, led by the Netaji, who were driven back from our North-east borders by the old British Raj, would be written in letters of gold.

I knew from talks to many survivors of the INA that they would have been happy if taken prisoner. They had never even thought of death but if it did overcome them, they had at least the satisfaction of having given their lives for their mother country. Withdrawn to Malaya, they were in a sorry plight. So were we all.

As for the masses in Malaya, nothing had yet happened to boost their morale. Most were fighting from day to day for mere subsistence. Those Chinese who had by now wormed their way into Japanese favour were nabobs of Malaya; others, whatever their creed, had sunk deeper in the gutter. People in Japanese-occupied Malaya then believed, or better still were made to believe, that the British had left for good. But then came the Jaywalk raid. A string of six laden cargo vessels, lying at anchor in the outer roads were mysteriously sunk one night. No enemy submarines or planes were reported in the area. The Japanese were completely baffled. Planes took off in all directions but no sign of the enemy. That he was somewhere near the Light of the South was evident to the Japanese as well as to all in the harbour who saw the hulks. It was equally evident to everybody in Malaya that the British were, after all, coming back.

It was only after Capt. Ivan Lyon's story was told following the war Malayans knew what was behind the mysterious explosions in Singapore Harbour. Lyon was itching to return to Singapore because he was forced to leave behind his wife and child when Singapore fell to Japanese. I do not know if he ever contacted his wife, then pining away in the PoW camp, but he did contact six Japanese vessels in Singapore Harbour of a total tonnage of 32,000 with TNT, or limpet mines.

It would be incorrect to say Indians were not thrilled by that long-distance strike. Every Indian was then in a mood to forget the fruitless march to Burma's western border. I wouldn't blame the Japanese for not doing their best for the INA. They could do nothing better in the circumstances. Gen. MacArthur was then gnawing at their vitals all along the Pacific islands reaching almost up to Japan itself.

From Burma it was not INA's retreat, but the first ever by Japan. She had, and I hope still has, the reputation of destroying the enemy when once encountered or falling in the encounter. Either this or that: there's no via media. Had it not been for the merciful Atom bomb I wonder if sons of the Sun-God would have been in existence now. The Atom is a twin-edged blade, one peaceful and the other martial. Strange as it may seem, the martial one had turned out to be humanity's saviour. How else could the world justify Hiroshima and Nagasaki?

It was a colossal massacre, I admit. What else is war? Those who dreaded massacre shouldn't have gone to war. They should have continued to make toys – oh, how elegant are Japanese contraptions! – while others went to war in 1939.

16

Death Railway

IN THE ARCHIVES of the Japanese High Command in Tokyo was pigeon-holed an old plan for building a link railway connecting the westernmost terminus of Thai Railways with the Burma Railways, the railroad passing through almost impossible primeval jungles over a distance of just over 100 miles at an elevation of over 3,000 feet. Expert topographical surveyors had been assisting the Japanese embassies in Bangkok and Rangoon for months before the outbreak of the Pacific was in charting a railway line across the border. On the Japanese annexation of Burma in April 1942, plans were set in motion to build this railway which was deemed an essential prerequisite for the invasion of India that had long dazzled the eyes of the military clique in Tokyo.

So, to the western border of Thailand were moved roughly five thousand British PoWs with double that number of an odd medley of Asians – Chinese, Malays, Indians and Eurasians. The former were billeted in a separate camp, and reputedly fed strictly according to the Geneva Convention. The men had to work from morn till eve, and had little time to clean their ulcers (known locally as jungle tumours) or wash their dirty, tattered garments.

Pernicious tropical ulcers which often began from a small scratch afflicted many, and limbs had to be amputated in hundreds of cases. And the sick-rooms were soon overcrowded.

A British doctor in charge of the camp told the Japanese commandant that unless each PoW was given twenty-six ounces of uncooked rice every day with adequate meat and vegetables the entire camp would be decimated by disease long before the railway line was completed. The commandant himself was stricken down by malaria one day, and the PoW doctor summoned to treat him gave him a shot of Atebrin which brought him round. Maybe out of gratitude, the doctor's request for increased rations was acceded to. And disease among PoWs fell correspondingly.

I met in Singapore – I'm sorry, Shonan – early in 1943 a Tokyo newsman who had been to Wampo and Tonchan in the Thai highlands where the PoWs were at work on the railway. He told me: 'Everything is progressing according to schedule.' (It was reminiscent of an army communiqué!) As I later learnt from the gist of my talk with this newsman, what he tried to convey to me was this: The whites were put to maximum work on the minimum food quota sanctioned by the Geneva Convention, and the Asians were well looked after. Sanitary facilities in the Asian camp were somewhat crude, but food was abundant, the newsman added. Although I had not visited the area, I gathered from passing Japanese journalists that both the camps, PoW and Asian, were nearly decimated by an outbreak of cholera. The leech, the mosquito and the Bengal tiger were the greatest enemies in these jungles. The *modus operandi* of the leech is most subtle. The Creator has given it the faculty of pole-vaulting over human flesh without in the least making it known that the worm is about to suck its victim's blood. It is a live needle that pierces your body after the point of puncture has been deadened by palliative like morphine. After it has had a square meal of your blood the blighter falls to the ground from the innermost recesses of your habiliments, if any. It has been long worshipped by jungle tribes as a discerning doctor. Anyway, practising leech craftsmen say it is a boon to mankind. But I wonder if it can distinguish between good and bad blood.

The mosquito is a more acknowledged enemy of mankind. One in three of the casualties among railway workers was traceable to malaria. From what I heard from the survivors, the tiger – Bengal, Burma or Thai – generally leaves things as they are, so long as it is left undisturbed or its stomach is not unduly lean. On the whole the jungle campers were left unmolested by the tiger. But a few Asian parties that attempted to escape by jungle trails were never heard of again. Whether tigers were on their trail none can say with any degree of certainty. Tiger footprints were clearly discernible on both sides of the track but never did they approach a camp site. As man slips down the ladder of civilisation it will not be long before man and beast are on nodding terms on the same rung!

One or two makeshift bridges gave way as the first train ran on the newly laid track. Dr Stanley Pavillard, a young physician from the Canary Islands who was in charge of nearly 1,500 prisoners at Camp Wampo, says[1] wooden bridges had been built clumsily from jungle trees, and the men who built them had taken every opportunity for sabotage. This is a statement with which few who knew the Japanese at the time will agree. As a rule they were whole-hoggers. They would hardly be satisfied with the look of a bridge; rather, each of the supports – however spick-and-span it might seem – was minutely examined to see that the spikes and belts were not put in wrong places. If any accidents occurred on the line due to structural defects the Japanese technicians who inspected the line might be asked to commit *harakiri*, or be disembowelled or shot. And the white contingent who built the line would be severely punished.

First steps of the project began in Shonan soon after the British retreat from Burma in April 1942 when PoWs were told they were to be moved overland to a higher elevation where the climate was less oppressive. Their hopes of spending some time in the Cameron Highlands faded when the PoW train steamed north of Selangor. They were taken out to the western terminal of Thai Railways, and from there batches of white PoWs and a mixed crowd of Asian labourers disappeared into the jungles to blaze a trail to Japan's new frontier. Nearly a third of the work parties perished from malaria, malnutrition, cholera or varying degrees of avitaminosis, particularly beri-beri and the dreaded pellagra. Besides, many had acute bacillary and amoebic dysentery, not to mention big tropical ulcers. Many somehow made their back to

---

1 Vide his book *Bamboo Doctor*: St. Martin's Press, London.

Singapore, an emaciated, tattered lot, and were later removed to Korea or Taiwan.

By the close of 1943, the defeated INA had been withdrawn to Malaya and Singapore from Burma, and for the first time the Japanese Navy failed to deliver the goods because of the repeated mauling it had had in the Coral Sea, Midway, Guadalcanal, Rabaul, the Marshalls and Truk (New Guinea). So, Pearl Harbour was not a death blow; it, on the other hand, helped to redouble America's was effort. By the summer of 1942 the Manhattan District Engineers, as the atom bomb's builders were called, had been given top priority. And by the middle of 1945 an invisible compound of equations, theory and scientific faith had been transformed into a practical military weapon that would eventually defeat Japan. But that kind of providential redemption was a long way off, three-and-a-half years of occupation actually, for Malaya and Singapore, doomed by Thailand's acquiescence to Japanese aggressive policies from the very beginning.

Thai Prime Minister Pibul Songkram had been pursuing a subtle policy that left the Japanese in utter dismay. They could not believe that Thailand would willingly be an ally of Japan before defeating Britain and the United States despite there being two factors in their favour. First, a common religion, Buddhism, united both the peoples in unbreakable bonds. Secondly, Japan's cheap manufactured goods were avidly sought after in Thailand. For toys, textiles and books imported from Western countries Thailand was paying nearly four or five times as much as it had to pay for the same things from Japan. Aversion to the West was at its zenith then.

If Japan had entered into diplomatic negotiations with Thailand before commencing operations she would have been forced to show her hand prematurely. This was indeed fatal to her designs. So, simultaneously with the 25th Army's landing at Singora, Patani and Kota Bharu, the once Imperial Guards Division (under the over-all command of Lt.-Gen Lida's 15th Army,) broke through the Indo-China-Thai border and advanced on Bangkok without encountering serious opposition. By noon the following day (Dec 9) its leading units had arrived at a position a few miles from the Thai capital. The army halted here, pending the result of its envoy's contact with Bangkok, but the car in which the envoy, Major Take-ne-Uchi, was travelling to the capital was ambushed by an angry crowd of Thai troops and civilians. The major was pulled out of the car and literally torn to pieces. He became the first Japanese casualty in the Pacific war. Militarists still bow before the urn in which his ashes are kept in the Yasukuni Shinto shrine[2] in Tokyo, moved there from a Buddhist temple in Kyoto, and worship Take-ne-Uchi as a demigod. No greater honour for a Japanese.

Thereupon the Japanese army brushed aside all opposition and advanced to the Thai capital. It was Buddhism that saved Bangkok from fruitless bloodshed. On Dec 11 the Thai Premier and Japanese Ambassador Tsubogami reached agreement on a Thai–Japanese Treaty which was formally signed in Bangkok

---

2 Enshrines Japanese who died in wars, including the military.

on Dec 21. By this time nearly a fortnight had elapsed since the war began in Malaya, and the Thai Government had had an opportunity to assess the war situation correctly.

The terms of the Thai–Japanese Treaty were as follows:

'For the Governments of the Empire of Japan and the Kingdom of Thai the establishment of a new order in East Asia is the only road to the prosperity of Eastern Asia.

'This agreement is made in the belief that the above named Governments have the firm will and the ability to eliminate all sources of trouble between them and that restoration of unconditional world peace is an essential matter.

Article 1: 'An alliance is established between the two countries, Japan and Thailand, as the foundation for respect of sovereignty and mutual independence.

Article 2: 'If either party is involved in military dissension with a third party, Japan and Thailand as allied powers agree to help each other by every kind of political, military and economic means.

Article 3: 'Matters which become operative under Article 2 shall be determined by a conference between the Government Agencies in Japan and Thailand having power to deal with the matters in question.

Article 4: 'In the event of Japan and Thailand becoming involved in collaboration in hostilities no peace or truce shall be made except in accordance with mutual agreement.

Article 5: 'The Treaty becomes effective simultaneously with signatures on behalf of the two powers and it will remain valid for ten years. The contracting countries shall consult each other about renewal of the treaty at an appropriate time before the expiration of the aforesaid period.'

I have reproduced the full text of the treaty because little was known about it in the outside world at the time. It gave legal right to Japan to link by rail Thailand with Burma. Even before the capture of Rangoon the Japanese High Command took preliminary steps to extend westward the Thai railways. And with the capture of Rangoon in April 1942, work was begun in earnest on the rail link. The INA's withdrawal from India's north-eastern borders in 1943, however, occurred at the same time as the reappearance of the Americans in the Pacific. What started as island-hopping in the Pacific was soon to blossom forth as a full-scale invasion of the Philippines in 1944 followed by Okinawa, culminating in the nuclear bombing of Hiroshima and Nagasaki.

Due to the very heavy casualties among the Burma railway workers, most present-day writers qualify this rail project which has since fallen into desuetude with the epithet 'Death'. That is more than justified, although the Japanese themselves, at the time bristling with war mania, did not quite realise the magnitude of the price the PoWs and others had to pay. Nearly twenty-five per cent of the entire construction gang left their bones in Thai or Burma jungles. A batch of INA survivors who traversed the jungle railway track in October 1943 told me on their return to Singapore that skeletal remains could often be seen on either side. The Asian workers had greater freedom than the PoWs and so they managed to buy food from the locals. But disease, not hunger, was their greatest enemy. Death Railway survivors I met in Singapore were mostly hospital cases, suffering from ghastly tropical ulcers. Their chins supported by emaciated hands, fingers reduced to matchsticks, they rarely touched on living conditions in the jungle camps. They evaded such painful questions. When cholera broke out in the Asian camp – nearly a hundred were buried in a common grave – a party of ten was went in search of a Thai medicine-man living in the foothills. They were never heard of again. Either they died of exhaustion or they fell to beasts of prey.

I met a Chinese survivor of the Death Railway in Singapore four years ago. He is a building contractor with a fat bank balance. He had four wives, each housed separately with her own brood. At tea, I asked him about his adventure, not travail, in Thailand in 1942. In gentle, well-modulated tones the towkay replied: 'Dear friend, who worries about yesterday or tomorrow so long as you are inextricably bound up with today? Yesterday is dead and gone. Tomorrow may never come to me, or to you for that matter. Then why worry?'

Echoes of Omar Khayyam. I am impressed.

17

A Present

THIS YEAR of grace 1944 was rung in with a great deal of Japanese jubilation. At the year-end banquet at Domei House *sake* flowed liberally and the Japanese spoke with spirit on the advent of their pet child, the Greater East Asia Co-Prosperity Sphere, whose main tenet was the giving away of food and clothes to every non-Anglo–American so long as he or she continued to be in the Axis camp. Once you stepped outside the sacred Axis alliance you were ripe for annihilation. Those utterances were made with missionary zeal and so were they publicized with the piety and devotion due to an extreme unction. Some cargo boats carrying iron-ore from Borneo to Japan were intercepted by the US Navy and sunk within a few miles of Mindanao. War production was being seriously interfered with and foreheads were seriously wrinkled in Tokyo. Many a service chief was recalled to Tokyo for urgent consultations. The man-in-the-street in Singapore could discern the rapid disappearance from the city of some key officers. Where were they going?

My old friend Nagai left his Penang assignment to his assistant and came to Singapore for further orders. He knew he was to go to the Philippines as an information officer. When he met me at dinner in a Chinese restaurant in South Bridge Road he told me of a sudden change of his assignment. On being asked where he was going in such haste, Nagai did not disclose his destination but politely said it was yet to be ascertained on his return to Tokyo. His main business with me that evening was to say goodbye and to give me a present. He had brought a dozen tweed suits from Penang, neatly packed in a trunk. And he wanted me to accept them as a memento of our short association in Malaya. I knew the Japanese would consider it an insult if a gift was totally rejected. Also, few at the time were brave enough to go about in tweeds except those in the higher cadre of service under the Japanese. So, just so as not to hurt him I selected a coffee-coloured shirt, and with bowing courtesy asked him to give away the rest to his other friends in Singapore. In thousands of military dollars, he settled the hotel bill, and by 9pm we emerged from the stifling atmosphere of the hotel.

From his demeanour, I suspected he didn't quite like the way I wriggled out of his immense sartorial presentation. But time was running out and he had to leave the island early the following morning. He hugged me and with tears in his eyes bade me a ceremonial goodbye. *Sayonara!*

After the war I heard that he fell in Leyte in November 1944. He is deified to this day in a Buddhist shrine at his home in Nagoya. He stood by Jose and me through thick and thin. Nagai's greatest asset when I knew him in Malaya was that he was less insular or more accommodating than most Japanese of the time.

He was not as stark mad as the bulk of his countrymen were at the time. I think of him not as a Japanese but as a large-hearted Asian. He loved his own country more than anything in the world but admitted there might be others as great as, if not more powerful than, Japan. Being a moderate, he would have preferred trade to war, but all this was well hidden once the militarists came to power in Tokyo. Had Nagai lived to the end of the war, he was the type that would have committed *harakiri* on Japan's surrender in August 1945.

I expected a British landing in Sumatra or Java by the time the Americans were well poised for an attack on Japanese-held Philippines. British operations in the Arakans in Burma, as I saw them through my short-sighted glasses in Japanese-held Singapore, were a blind to a major offensive that was expected to arise south of Singapore. Both these expectations were belied by later developments, and we were spared from a vicious vice which would have engulfed Singapore. That was why I decided in 1944 to get out of Singapore. I feigned illness in office one morning early in 1944 and I was immediately sent to hospital. The Japanese doctor recommended to Domei that I might be moved to a hill resort for a short period of rest and recuperation. It was thus that I arranged my get-away from Singapore whose one million civilian population would have been annihilated if the British or Americans had made a landing either in Malaya or in the present Indonesia. After a few weeks Jose, too, was transferred to the Domei office in Kuala Lumpur, just to look after me in my convalescence.

Thus we two fled the city, Jose to Kuala Lumpur and I to Fraser's Hill to recover from neurosis which my doctor feared might lead to cerebral thrombosis unless I strictly adhered to the drugs he prescribed. First I thought I had nicely hoodwinked the doctor but after a fortnight of brooding at the hill station I began to fear the doctor might have been right after all! Wasn't there a little stiffness in the joints? From then on I followed the doctor's instructions rigorously. I felt immensely better after the spell on Fraser's Hill. My prayers were answered when I was posted to the Domei office in Kuala Lumpur.

Since the INA's withdrawal from the Burma frontier in the last quarter of 1943 the Japanese did not attach much importance to my daily broadcasts to India. In the circumstances, my absence passed off without much comment in Shonan Domei. At this period, a Japanese newsman acted as my proxy in Shonan. My assignment in Kuala Lumpur was only of a consultative capacity. I had little to do besides okaying the daily newscasts sent out from the office, spending the leisure hours chewing the cud. What next? Although no gunfire was heard in Singapore or Malaya the warfront in the world at large was suddenly turning to the advantage of the Allies. Island-hopping by the Americans had progressed by leaps and bounds. Japanese supplies to the their forces in the Philippines, which was then under the command of General Yamashita, the conqueror of Singapore, were at this time seriously affected by American air and submarine strikes. The common man in Japan raised his eyebrows at the swift approach of Anglo–Americans to their prime target – Japan.

Japan had completely miscalculated the pace of American recovery from Pearl Harbour. According to their own estimates, it might have taken at least seven years for the Americans to replace their Pacific Fleet, the bulk of which was sent to the bottom on Dec 7, 1941. Yet in April 1945 the Japanese High Command must have been dismayed to see the greatest naval armada in history – one thousand and three hundred ships transporting 183,000 assault troops – converge on Okinawa, a lizard-shaped island south of Japan. And this after General Eisenhower's liberation army had been fighting in Europe for more than nine months and was well in sight of final victory. Hitler and his mistress, Eva Braun, committed suicide on April 30, 1945, while the US armada was grappling with the tenacious Japanese in Okinawa. In roughly twelve weeks of fighting in Okinawa no less than 110,000 Japanese were smoked out of limestone caves and killed in the fiercest of encounters in the Pacific. Even with the assemblage of such an immense fleet for the reduction of a sixty-mile stretch of coral reef, two to fifteen miles wide, the American casualties mounted to more than 49,000 in Okinawa alone. How much more would the casualties mount if the next logical step, invasion of the Japanese home islands, were to come about? This was the main consideration that weighed with the Allied leaders at Potsdam when they issued an ultimatum to Japan. It demanded that Japan surrender or be crushed, promised Japan would not be destroyed as a nation, and hinted that the Emperor would be left on the throne. By accident or design, Japan ignored the ultimatum. And Hiroshima and Nagasaki were the result.

Meanwhile Jose and I were building castles in the air, looking for the lightest ray to illuminate the gloom enveloping us. As we heard of the Normandy invasion, one month after the Allied forces landed on the French coast, we knew our pet idea of a British thrust on Indonesian coast had to be abandoned once and for all. It was clear that no such operation was likely to take place before a decision was reached in Europe. All the same, the American drive in the Pacific, from island to island, was gaining in strength. Having mostly relied on British sources for our education and upbringing, we could not believe at that time the Americans were strong enough to carry by themselves the war burden in the Pacific. Yet, by the end of the year (1944), General MacArthur drove into the Philippines, liberating the entire island community by early February the following year. By that time General Eisenhower's Allied forces had liberated France and had driven deep into western Germany. And by early May 1945 the Reichstag in Berlin was razed to the ground by Russian bombs, and with the Allies in the west and Russians in the east, Berlin was caught in a murderous vice. The agony ended on May 5, 1945.

By the time the Philippine islands were liberated, we blinked our eyes in Japanese occupied Southeast Asia and could dimly discern the outlines of a new military power emerging into the world arena, the United States of America, whose full stature was yet to be gauged. Our sympathies were for the Americans because we knew they would have to make colossal sacrifices if they alone were to attempt to liberate every occupied country in East Asia. In Japanese eyes they were waging a war, a holy war, for the redemption of Asians from the Anglo–American yoke. And we knew no country could be re-conquered until not only the Japanese forces but the bulk of the Asian population were also wiped out in the process. Would the Americans make this colossal sacrifice?

However much Domei strove to suppress from the people of occupied countries the daily developments, by early July it was known to everybody that Hitler's wonted European fortress had been broken by Allied forces. We naturally expected an Allied liberation army to try and recover so strategic a point as Singapore, but other facets of war strategy conspired to give the heart of Japan priority over every other area. So, from the Philippines the US carried the war via Okinawa right to the heart of Japan: Hiroshima and Nagasaki. And thank God we were left severely alone.

Redemption was still fourteen months away. The crisis then facing the civilian population, or rather the problems of the present, were much harsher than those that confronted us in 1941-1942. Due to increasing hazards the coastal trade with both Indo-China and Thailand was rapidly petering out to nothingness, leaving the rail link with Bangkok as the only source of Malaya's rice. And of Malaya's civilian population which at that time amounted roughly to six million only one-sixth could be fed by the country's own rice output. The balance had to be fed from extraneous sources. It was at this time that Malaya learned to appreciate the resourcefulness and never-failing vigour of Malayan Chinese entrepreneurs. By sampan or junk they brought rice from Saigon and Bangkok and, with or without Japanese connivance, sold off the stock at fantastic prices (in honest-to-goodness Straits dollars). Cartloads of military scrip were dumped on Singapore at the time; by devious ways they found their way ultimately to latrines all over the country. School children collected bagfuls of military scrip and played rich, even while they were forced to subsist upon a single meal of tapioca gruel with a teaspoonful of rice and fish paste a day.

Now that the war did not appear to go Japan's or INA's way, food had become a national preoccupation. Even our rations had to be cut whenever American submarines got the better of the Japanese Navy and sank coastal steamers carrying rice to Malaya. Distress was widespread, and yet most people clung fast to their hidden gold, which alone could save them in the end. Most of Domei's typist girls carried their gold, as I found out after the war, secreted as thin sheets in the soles of their shoes. Most of them survived the war without having to demolish their soles!

18

Survival

THE LIBERATION of France in 1944 after the Normandy landings went by almost unnoticed in Shonan. Any reference to it in Domei reports was often qualified by the remark that the Nazis were merely waiting for the entire Allied forces to land in France before some fictional pincers would close in on them. Well, people in Axis-occupied countries of Asia, Africa and Europe already knew the importance of keeping our mouths shut, whichever way the wind blew. There was no mercy for those caught rumour-mongering. In Nazi occupied countries they would be sent to concentration camps, infinitely worse than being shot dead at first sight, to wither away to bleached bones. Just being a Jew was a death sentence in any Nazi-occupied territory, in Italy the victims were so-called 'anti-Fascists', in Japanese-occupied countries anyone branded a Communist was killed right away or sent to work on the Death Railway.

It was sheer necessity that drove Communist Party of Malaya secretary-general Chin Peng and his band into the jungles in 1942. Apart from the constant threat of being rounded up and killed, there were no jobs to make a living. The most lucrative profession was that of the market gardener. He would raise two or three crops of paddy in addition to a variety of vegetables and fruits. The catch was that not everyone was allowed to indulge in this new-found interest in growing things. The Japanese decreed that the white collar or clerical classes had to rejoin their offices. If their old avenues of employment no longer existed they were given jobs in Japanese agencies. Most men without any ostensible means of livelihood were rounded up by military police and sent to work on the Thai-Burma railway. This was tantamount to a death sentence.

As the war intensified in Europe and the Pacific, things became difficult in Shonan. Most were subsisting on a single meal of tapioca and weak rice gruel. When even tapioca became unavailable, teenagers raided restaurants all over Malaya that were still open under Japanese auspices. Those caught were beheaded in public squares.

In the cities and towns practically the entire civilian population, men, women, and children were out on the streets hawking whatever they possessed for a morsel of food. Judging by their clothes, no one could say they were in utter privation. Most men and women on the streets were well dressed, thanks to the bad old colonial days. Few Asians had the patience to extract some news from the daily Domei newscasts that might suggest an early end to their distress. The final news round-up of December, 1944, was indeed hopeful to the Allies. But the Malayan of the day who well knew the Japanese methods at close quarters couldn't by any stretch of the imagination be persuaded to believe that the down-fall of the Axis was near at hand. The Japanese military strategists had calculated that an enemy landing force approaching anywhere near the Japanese occupied regions could be detected at least a hundred miles off the possible landing point, and that it could almost be decimated before it ever reached land. Everybody who watched the spectacular drive of Japanese forces from Patani right down to Singapore in bare seventy days, a distance of roughly 500 miles, well knew the immensity of danger that confronted an invader. The insuperable difficulties that lay in the path of reannexing the vast regions in Southeast Asia that fell to Japan in 1941-42 were quite apparent to both sides. But the future, then as now, was a closed book. All of us were neatly squeezed through a bottle neck.

Towards the end of 1942 I was able to send a brief message to my wife, through the good offices of a Japanese friend, who transmitted it to India via the International Red Cross in Geneva. In it I said: 'Jose and I very much alive and kicking.' My wife who was, on the other hand, fed on British propaganda from New Delhi could hardly believe we were still alive. We might have been burnt to cinder in the fierce bombing of Singapore or, at best, might have survived only to perish by starvation. Though she could hardly believe that the Red Cross cable was mine, it later dawned on her that nobody else in Malaya knew her correct home address in India. So, immediately she replied to me by cable via the Red Cross: 'All well with us.' I do not know how long it remained in the hands of the censorship board in Tokyo but it did reach me at Shonan Domei Thushin-sya in August 1944. Whisky or *sake* couldn't be had then; so a bottle of Chinese *samsu* sufficed to celebrate. What a stimulant that brief note from India was! Surprisingly enough, the message to my wife was also broadcast by All-India Radio. I am certain that SEAC HQ knew at the time who the author of the Singapore broadcasts beamed at India was.

As for the British, I can tell from my own experience, as an erstwhile colonial under them, that they know, or rather knew, very well how to rule you without your knowing that you are an underdog. That is a sort of anaesthetic which the British used with circumspection to prolong the life of their British Empire for one hundred and fifty years or so.

The decolonisation move that started with India's independence twenty years ago is still continuing. And it may be conjecture that before this century is out the British would bow out of every Asian and African territory that is still under their tutelage. As I see it, Hong Kong is an exception, as Portuguese Macao is. Would the Chinese rather leave them alone because these two territories are the eyes and ears of communist China today? Perhaps, they are proving a headache to China today. The moment the United States Seventh Fleet moves away, if ever it would, communist China would devour Taiwan in one gulp.

In normal times the average Chinese would have gone to the nearest opium den to smoke out his misery. But in wartime opium was not available except to the very, very rich. A few medicine-men in Singapore's Chinatown who cornered the market as the Japanese invaders entered Selangor sold the drug at such exorbitant prices as to make them inordinately rich overnight.

Their harems, too, multiplied at the same pace, and I have heard that each of the new rich had as much as ten to fifteen wives, the youngest being hardly twelve or thirteen. Had it not been for the difficulty in feeding them, the strings of aspiring wives crowding at the gates of these nabobs would have lengthened farther. Food was the acutest problem to all but those who worked for the Japanese. Fortunately, Asia's rice bowl was at the time under Japanese occupation. And whenever wagons could be released, we could get as much rice as we needed from Bangkok. But detectives were employed to find out any diversion to unauthorised persons. And if any were caught black-marketing in rice the hapless man's or woman's head would be on public display in the *padangs* or market squares. But how did six unemployed out of every ten in Singapore subsist? The Japanese fed 400,000 in Singapore, but what about the remaining 600,000?

In normal times, a discreet newsman would have revealed astonishing details of how those people filled their stomachs every day. But not with a war on. The landed gentry in the north was fairly well off. As soon as their rubber was tapped, coagulated, and dried it was sold on barter for rice to Japanese merchants, and it was soon laden for Yokohama. Indians on the mainland tapped the rubber trees to slaughter in return for wages in rice. Most of the remaining Indians were associated in some way to the INA and were looked after by the powers that be.

The Malay population fell back on their farms as they did before the British and the rubber tree invaded their country early in the nineteenth century. Thus the Malays largely escaped the ravages of war. But the Chinese were largely unattended to. In Singapore city there were roughly 800,000 Chinese of whom only a small proportion was absorbed in Japanese service. Barring the few who collaborated with the Japanese in running cabarets or 'all-night' resting places, which was another name for simple whore-houses, almost half a million Chinese had to find rice for themselves. It was fascinating to delve into the methods by which they did so.

There were roughly 50,000 Japanese stationed in Singapore. All the army, navy, and air force canteens were run by Chinese *amahs* with a veritable army of Chinese assistants. The big shots of the services lived in separate bungalows exclusively serviced by Chinese. Thus it was that at least 200,000 Chinese were fed daily from the largesse of these establishments. An amah, or maid-servant, working in a Japanese army mess in Johore was known to have been feeding a hundred relatives. In Malaya, the Chinese mostly looked northward into the sea for their fishing craft, which would unload rice, not fish, at night.

Time was when China had to feed a Japanese army to fight against her! She is too vast a land mass of Asia that a few more or fewer millions to feed was, apparently, not much of a problem. And if driven to the wall, the Chinese knew how either to demolish the wall or to annihilate the enemy from behind. It was China's immensity in area and population that prevented Japan from devouring her in the Thirties. But during the Japanese occupation of Malaya (1942-45) the plight of Chinese was entirely different. The area in which they could move about was very much restricted, and the curfew regulations were so strict that movement at night was well-nigh impossible. If a Chinese were caught on the streets at night, he would instantly be slashed to pieces by the sword which every Japanese carried as an embellishment to his modern arms. Chinese youths who didn't want to be burden upon their families in those days of acute stress, therefore, followed the trail to the jungles. They hid themselves in mountain fastnesses and pillaged neighbouring villages in the plains at night.

The Allied landing in Normandy in June 1944 was instantly known in Singapore's underworld. And since the later liberation of Paris, Malayans generally were unwilling to sell anything for Japanese scrip. Transactions, if any, were reduced to barter or Straits currency. On the other hand, all merchants were eager to unload cartloads of military dollars (called colloquially as banana notes) if they could get something worth while. By the end of 1944, the monetary situation threatened to defy the sword which it almost did by the middle of the following year when Nazi Germany had surrendered to the Allies.

19

Prayer Censor

WE HAD already celebrated two new years under the Japanese – 1943 and 1944 – and on both occasions the Japanese employers had assembled their staff in the central halls of their offices for speeches in Nippon-go on the Co-Prosperity Sphere. This was defined as the new symbol of Asia, a new forward move by hitherto enslaved Asians under Japanese auspices. In simple words, it meant the diversion of the occupied region's entire trade to Japan who, in return, would exclusively meet all the import needs of the region. There was no longer any need for Asian peoples to knock on the doors of western nations, so we were told, whenever they required bicycles, pharmaceuticals, cosmetics or textiles.

Nippon-jin (the Japanese) are predestined to look after not only the millions of China but of every other country from Manchukuo to Burma. The British colonialists are still holding out in India. Our next major move would be against British India, and then against China, the only segments of Asia that are still under foreign domination. (Indians, at this stage, had to shout again and again 'Challo Dilli!' with clenched fists in the air, although the war-cry had lost its sting with the retreat of the INA from Imphal.)

'Let's pray for our departed brethren.' All would then join in chanting, not shouting as was the custom in the two previous years, '*Banzai*' to Emperor Hirohito, turning towards Tokyo.

That was the gist of Japanese speech-making on ceremonious occasions. Unlike the two previous new years, 1945 opened rather unceremoniously with the precipitate switching off of electric lights all over the country. The new year ceremonies were restricted to a brief turning north-eastward to Tokyo and chanting '*Banzai*' a few times. Everybody knew there was something wrong somewhere. But nothing could be gauged from Japanese physiognomy. It was as inscrutable as ever. If anything, they seemed to be moving about with a design; what it was nobody could fathom.

Almost the first thing the Japanese did on Singapore's surrender in 1942 was the impounding of all radios in the possession of non-Japanese. Yet, tanks to the Chinese underworld, there were a few radio sets which gave their lucky owners daily news of the war-torn world.

By early 1945, the Americans were distinctly on the offensive in the Pacific although at a lesser pace than in Europe. It was fairly evident the previous December that the Americans were going straight for Japan's throat without frittering away their energies in a long drawn-out war in the East Indies or Malaya. The Philippines was on the road to Tokyo, and so they were annexed in February 1945 by General MacArthur. Like General Eisenhower's in Normandy, his was a name fast rising in the Pacific. France's redemption from Nazi occupation in the last quarter of 1944, followed by the Allied crossing of the Maginot Line[1] had brought the Americans and the British into Western Germany while the Soviet Army steamrolled into the country from the east. The Nazi armies had almost lost hope since their debacle in Stalingrad. From then on it was only a matter of time for the two Allied prongs to close in on Berlin. When Soviet bombs were pulverising the outer ramparts of the Reichstag, Hitler and his mistress took their own lives. And all was over within a week in Europe.

Meanwhile MacArthur overran the Philippines, and General Yamashita, the conqueror of Singapore in 1942, who was in overall command of the Philippines at the time, was taken prisoner by the American forces and executed a few months later. With lightning speed news spread throughout the country, although only discerning readers of Domei newscasts could decipher them and arrive at nearly correct conclusions. For instance, a month after America's re-occupation of the Philippines naval base, Corregidor, and the capture of General Yamashita, master of the 70-day campaign through Malaya which culminated in the seizure of the fortress of Singapore, the Shonan *Shimbun* published a story on how the Imperial Japanese Army, in active co-operation with the Navy, repelled an American night invasion of Luzon. A Japanese communiqué said: 'An American night invasion was beaten off Luzon with awesome losses to the enemy. Hundreds of enemy

---

[1] Heavy fortifications created by France along the German border which, in the event, worked both ways.

planes were shot down and thousands of naval units spearheaded by landing craft sunk so much so that our reconnaissance planes could not find any sign of activity in American bases in the Pacific.' Like the death of Admiral Isoroku Yamamoto, C-in-C of the Japanese Navy, when his plane was shot down by Americans off Bougainville, the shooting of The Tiger (General Yamashita) was hidden from the public until the Americans broke the news. Similarly, there had been a succession of loss of face prior to Japan's unconditional surrender.

By and by, it became known that the end of Japan's military clique was only a matter of months. And there was a mad hunt for mementoes – from army headgear and swords of those who committed *harakiri* right down to turkey-towels, a vital part of the Japanese soldier's accoutrements. For myself, I was eager to acquire a Japanese censored *Book of Common Prayer* of the Church of England. In 1942, the Kempeitai had asked for a senior Japanese subeditor from Domei to assist a committee which was then set up to blur out in indian ink certain objectionable passages from the Bible and the Book of Common Prayer before they were distributed to PoWs. After the dirty work was done Nagai confided in me that he would some day ask the commander of Changi Jail, where the prisoners were interned, to let me have one of the holy books 'when all's over'.

In the third week of August 1945 when nobody knew what would befall the Shonan fortress, I plucked up courage to contact the commander at Changi by telephone. Although the howl at the other end somewhat unnerved me, I asked the official if he could redeem the late Nagai's pledge to me. It was surprising that Colonel Kobayashi suddenly calmed down and, with uncommon courtesy, asked me to call at Changi 'whenever you like and collect whatever you want'. Agreeably surprised, I thanked the colonel and replaced the receiver. I visited his bungalow the following day, and Kobayashi searched through his bric-a-brac and handed me a dog-eared copy of *Common Prayer with Hymns: Ancient and Modern of the Church of England*. The hymns escaped virtually unmolested but the *Book of Common Prayer* came under greater scrutiny and almost every other page was heavily blotted out. I still keep it as a valuable curio.

I wonder if 'RSH' is still alive; he must be a very brave man indeed to have jotted down, in some sort of prison-made ink, '*In the name of RSH*' after '*Glory be to the Father, and to the Son, and to the Holy Ghost.*' After chanting the morning prayer or the psalms every day throughout the 3½-year occupation RSH quills, or should it be quilled, '*No pardon whatsoever for idolaters*' with the date and exact time of the entry. I can well imagine the hope not unmixed with turmoil in the mind of RSH when he underlined the following words in Benedictus (St. Luke 1:68) at 6.37am on Dec. 30, 1944:

'Blessed be the Lord God of Israel: for He hath visited, and redeemed His people;

'And hath raised up a mighty salvation for us: in the house of His servant David;

'As He spake by the mouth of His holy prophets: which have

been since the world began;

'That we should be saved from our enemies: and from the hands of all that hate us.'

Yes, RSH's redemption from his enemy was near at hand at the time. That is the story of the late Nagai's parting bequest to me.

As the story of the sudden end of the European segment of the Axis trio, leaving Japan as the sole adversary in the field, spread in Asia there was some sort of leave-taking among civilians. What appeared early as a faint glint in the dark clouds overhanging us had generally been accepted as widening, and the end of the war was almost within sight but to those of us who were familiar with Japanese thinking knew that the Japanese would rather die at their post than meekly give in to the Allies. Anyway, the subdued nightlong feasting in Chinatown restaurants was noticed by others. But the cat was not yet out of the bag. Some who feared that the Japanese would burn the entire city kept a vigil every night. But nothing untoward happened, thank God. After Japan's surrender was broadcast by Tokyo the sons of Sun-God hardly came out of their rent-free houses, and in a few weeks ship-loads were dispatched to Japan.

The staggering casualties that were expected if an invasion of Japan were attempted might have moved the Americans to try out the atom bomb prior to the invasion of the island empire scheduled for November. The bombs had their desired effect and the Japanese sued for peace within days. The thing had happened so suddenly that only the following month did we come out of our burrows for the first time since the guns of Singapore were silenced in 1942. Ah, a new lease of life.

But in the few weeks prior to everything being silenced in Japan, I went through the severest mental agony ever experienced in the 3½-year interregnum. Should Jose and I again flee Singapore? This was a question that nagged my brain day and night. How another 'convalescence' was engineered I shall relate in the penultimate chapter. Work in Domei offices was creaking to a stop. Typing, subbing, okaying and distribution of newscasts ceased because Tokyo news could not be picked up. Girls took hours in the bathroom (powdering and re-powdering their noses to greet a new age!), boys chain-smoked, and the elderly reclined in blissful reverie. Everybody's problem was this: How to tide over the evening?

A detached observer of Japanese ups and downs during the occupation saw them in the clouds in 1942 and 1943, a little more visible and communicable in 1944, and like any of us, down-to-the-earth, earthy in the following year. It was indeed paying back in the same coin to see them cleaning the drains and roads before being taken to Changi Jail en route to General MacArthur's Japan. I heard that a few in Malaya committed ceremonial *harakiri* on hearing that the Son of Heaven had given himself up and his people to the Americans. Survivors among Japan's fighting services would marvel at Japan's ascendancy in the commercial world as the world's second largest exporter and Asia's foremost importer of iron-ore. Thanks to American perspicacity, Japan's genius today is wholly turned to commerce.

Japanese servicemen in Malaya seemed to be more purposeful than ever since the Axis surrender in Europe. They were ordered to stand where they were and resist the enemy whenever or wherever he touched the shore. Their old idol, General Yamashita[2], was an American prisoner in the Philippines and Japanese military propagandists urged their forces to annihilate the enemy whenever he might appear so that Yamashita might be rescued and the Fatherland preserved.

Life appeared to be rather free and easy in Singapore as well as on the mainland, especially since the beginning of May. 'Now we can very well afford to be alone in the world against Anglo–Americans. We press a button in Kyoto, and up goes American city after city in flames. Okinawa is teaching Anglo–American "devils" how bloody the road will be ... to the Japanese mainland. We shall destroy them before they can reach the shores of our Fatherland.' This was the gist of what a Japanese colleague of mine lectured me at the time. Although morale of sorts was maintained in occupied countries, back in Japan it was a different story following the capture of Okinawa by American forces. Tokyo sent unofficial feelers to Moscow seeking a 'decent' cessation of hostilities more than five weeks before the atomic attack. The Japanese Foreign Minister, Shigenori Togo, ordered his ambassador in Moscow, Naotake Sato, to raise the prospects for peace, maybe even Japan's surrender, with the Soviet Foreign Minister (Molotov). But the

---

2 He may have been executed by then.

Russians were rather lukewarm, saying they would 'consider Japan's suggestion' after the Potsdam conference.

Despite all the Japanese bluster in Singapore, we knew from the underworld that Moscow had brushed aside Japan's peace feelers, making an Allied invasion imminent. We all knew what would happen if the Allies did invade Singapore, although the absence of such an Allied or British invasion was widely misinterpreted among Asians. Japanese forces would, of course, be in the vanguard to resist the invader, with able-bodied civilians (men and women) as a second string, stiffened by an inner ring of *kamikaze*s. Why were civilians to be called out? Those who believed in the Co-Prosperity Sphere, which Japan was allegedly setting up with missionary zeal, had to fight for the cause, with or without arms!

In the circumstances, little wonder all who could afford to move upcountry did move away from Singapore under some pretext. In my case, the Domei chief suggested several times that I should get away to Kuala Lumpur to hasten my 'recovery'. Had he sensed the popular mood? I always felt there was a juvenile streak in the Japanese character, although it completely vanished once they marched into battle. On the battlefield, the Japanese did not fight for themselves but for *Tennv-Heika*, the Son of Heaven. His enemies were to be wiped out wherever encountered. It was this ardent zeal that fired Japanese as squad after squad of *kamikaze* pilots hurled themselves upon US ships as they converged on the Philippines and later on Okinawa.

The Axis Powers' surrender in Europe was, as one might

suspect, not an occasion for the eastern remnant of the Axis to be jubilant over. What, then, was the object of Japanese merrymaking? Invariably, the Japanese wore long faces on Mondays following the apparent weekend celebrities. I surmised they were not festivities in the real sense of the term but were merely escapist. They knew that not one of them would be alive if the Allies launched a full-scale invasion in strength. So they were making hay while the sun shone. The atom bomb and Japan's surrender following the incineration of more than 200,000 souls in an instant, never figured in anybody's calculation at the time. We the civilians as well as Japanese servicemen in Malaya expected an overwhelming Allied thrust on the shores of Malaya or Sumatra coupled with a landward thrust into west Burma from north-east India. So, the occupying power was just bidding us goodbye in their own way. They were still cruel to the last. Starvation and beatings and beheadings continued in prison camps.[3]

At this stage, the average Chinese and Indian in Malaya were fearful of the battles to come. But the face of the average Malay beamed in the expectation of redemption. The price he might have to pay did not cross his mind. In the event, his smiles were rewarded. Yes, the atom had done its trick, redeeming the world

---

3 A series of forced marches in Borneo from Sandakan to Renau resulted in the deaths of 2,345 British and Australian PoWs from Singapore. Prisoners who survived the brutal march were shot. The last shootings occurred 10 days after Japan's surrender. Six who escaped into the jungle were the only survivors from two camps.

of six years of 'blood, sweat, and toil' as Winston Churchill put it in a memorable speech.

20

Mokusatsu

NEWS TRAVELS from ear to ear with bewildering speed. By early May 1945 everybody in Japanese-occupied areas from Hong Kong to Rangoon knew of the unceremonious exit of Adolf Hitler and Benito Mussolini and the surrender of Nazi Germany and Fascist Italy, leaving Japan alone in the field against the Allied Powers. Though the English translations of Domei newscasts printed in Malayan newspapers did not contain any reference to the Axis surrender, about ten days after the event a Japanese commentator characterised Nippon as '*the lone* adversary of Anglo–Americans'. The cat was out of the bag.

The common man's first reaction was one of high elation but later he gave himself up to despair because the Samurai was never known to surrender. But Hideki Tojo's subsequent abandonment of Premiership and Kantora Suzuki's elevation as the new Prime Minister helped raise our hopes of some sort of cessation of hostilities with the Allies. As ever, practically nothing could be gauged from Japanese faces. And whenever they made a public pronouncement it was common for them to assert that 'the Co-Prosperity Sphere had come to stay, whatever might befall the

European twins of Axis'.

The Nazis surrendered to the Allies as the most crucial battle was being fought in the East China Sea for the island of Okinawa, gateway to Japan proper. Described as the greatest sea–air battle in history, Okinawa was a combined operation unparalleled in size, scope and ferocity. The Japanese lost nearly 10,000 planes and 110,000 killed. It was the staggering losses inflicted upon the enemy as well as those suffered by themselves, that ultimately weighed with the Americans in trying out the first atom bombs on Japan proper.

There were two schools of thought among civilians at the time. One was to be as near Singapore as circumstances permitted, and the other was to get as far away from that strategic base. It was widely held that the Americans would abruptly stop at Okinawa, giving the British an opportunity to reconquer Burma and Malaya, and the Dutch to reclaim their old East Indies. The secret atom bomb was then being created, and how effective it would turn out in forcing Japan to surrender almost unconditionally was not known even to its fathers, the Manhattan District Engineers. I was itching for news, so I hastened to Singapore on a week's holiday. What I detected there soon led me back to Kuala Lumpur.

After nearly twelve hours' run my train steamed into the Singapore station at dawn on May 20, 1945. Unlike in normal times, the station appeared to be deserted. The lines of trishaws and taxi cabs had well-nigh disappeared. Nor could I find a man to carry my bag. On telephoning Domei, a car was sent to fetch me. At breakfast in the Domei mess I inadvertently asked a Japanese friend if it was true that Hitler and Mussolini were dead. As I knew him in normal times, Morokuma-san was the least unapproachable among the higher-ups but he was the very devil incarnated when I put that question to him. Arms swinging, he rose from his seat and told me to mind my own business which was to assimilate and then discharge Tokyo newscasts to local newspapers. He was diligently ploughing through an *ikan kurau*[1] with a sharp table knife when I, as he put it, raided him with an anti-Axis question.

'You value your life, don't you? So, mind your language, eh?' I fled to a friend's home in Singapore.

The city appeared to be very much alive and kicking. The three 'Worlds' – the Happy, the Great and the New – seemed to have touched a new high with 'dance as you sleep' and 'sleep as you dance' to Japanese lullabies. A brand of shady local Chinese was making capital out of Japanese weaknesses. Like bees, lured by flamboyant flowers, Japanese servicemen as well as civilians hovered about the cabarets late into the small hours of the morning. The shapely legs that swung before the public gaze might have gathered vital information for the Kempeitai. The informer and recipient would then retire into a secret apartment to talk over the coming day's assignments. Two or three girl informers who were suspected to be in secret liaison with Communists in the jungle were known to have been liquidated.

Since the surrender of the European wing of the Axis, the

---

1 Threadfin, a Malayan table fish.

Japanese never looked back. Although Tokyo made some overtures to Moscow, first, for some 'decent settlement' of the war and later for conditional surrender with unrestrained freedom for Japan to choose her own government and Emperor Hirohito to be left on the throne. But when the Potsdam Declaration was issued by Britain, the United States and China, promising that Japan would not be destroyed as a nation and accepting the two main terms she had demanded, the Militarists in Tokyo played a deft sleight-of-hand trick. Firstly, they wanted to ignore the ultimatum – it was only broadcast from London and New York, and not presented at the Imperial Palace in Tokyo. Two days after the ultimatum was issued the then Prime Minister of Japan (Kantaro Suzuki) announced that the cabinet intended to continue its policy of *mokusatsu*. This rare Nippon-go word, which is ambiguous even in the Japanese language, means either to ignore or accept, according to circumstances. It might also mean 'refrain from comment'. So, relying on Domei's translation of the word the British and American Press inferred that Japan was determined to fight on. The Allies' interpretation of Suzuki's statement of July 28, 1945, was exactly what the Japanese intended it to be. The result: atomic bombing, followed shortly by Japan's surrender.

From talks I had with friends in Singapore, I found that the bulk of public opinion was inclined to the view that the Japanese intended to continue fighting for every inch of space they were occupying, come what might. Japanese servicemen as well as civilians were asked to form an impregnable line of defence in coastal areas where the 'whites' might land. We were expecting a SEAC invasion from India under the overall command of Lord Mountbatten. But he did not have to order an invasion – the SEAC chief visited a quiet and peaceful Singapore within weeks of Japan's surrender.

Meanwhile, work in Domei offices was practically at a standstill. By the end of June the loss of the much-touted Okinawa was apparent to us by the disclosure that General Ushijima, who commanded Japanese troops in Okinawa, had resorted to ceremonial death by *harakiri*. It was all over bar the shouting because next on the Allied list was the southernmost 'home' island of Kyushu. Good sense triumphed in Tokyo by July but little could be done to save nearly a quarter of a million people who perished due to her own linguistic ambiguity, whether by design or accident – *mokusatsu* recoiled on them like a boomerang.

I noticed a change in the behaviour of Japanese working in the building, especially since the end of June. Hitherto none but those who were directly associated with what they called the English section condescended to talk to any of us. What I mean by 'us' is the group of locals who were indispensable in subbing, or rather deciphering, Tokyo English newscasts. About 15 local men and women worked with me on Domei – ten Chinese, a Filipino, two Ceylonese, one Eurasian and Jose. Surprising, but we were often asked to attend *sukiyaki* parties at Domei House in Singapore or Kuala Lumpur. Their final adieu to Malaya and Shonan or to the world?

Then suddenly all private merrymaking came to an abrupt stop. 'Confront the enemy wherever he may come from, and fight him with your backs to the wall. *Banzai* to *Tenno-Heika*!' So said an order of the day to his troops in the southern regions from Field Marshal Count Terauchi, Commander-in-Chief of the Southern Armies. Many a Japanese thereupon renounced liquor and cigarettes and, Buddha-like, sat cross-legged on the floor meditating upon the immediate future. Krishna could have joined them, because his own duties were becoming impossible to fulfil. It was difficult to buy anything with military scrip unless accompanied by a Samurai sword. The unarmed man with a cartload of banana notes couldn't buy a cup of *kopi-o*. He would be lucky to escape unharmed.

Almost at the same time many a secret hoard surfaced. It would have dumbfounded the Japanese had they seen the immense wealth – gold, silver and straits currency – emerging from the heart of the community as Japanese defeat seemed certain. By July all private transactions were in Straits currency while mountains of military scrip lay abandoned in every godown. Millions of dollars worth of textiles, liquor, cosmetics and so on were available in every town on the mainland as well as in Singapore if one knew where to look, and what coin to pay in.

Work in the office was rather light these days. Normally we would receive rigorously censored English newscasts from Tokyo but for four or five days in the second week of August – now I know it was all because of the atom bomb – we had no news from Tokyo Domei at all. The Japanese cooked up a long serial yarn on 'the crippling blow administered to the US Navy in the outer approaches to Okinawa' and other Japanese victories in Java,

Burma and other war theatres. Like Kitchener in Khartoum or the historic Charge of the Light Brigade, I knew the Japanese in Malaya were planning to steel themselves four-square and fight to the bloody end. They knew there was no escape and I do not think they would have taken advantage of any avenue of escape because their Samurai concept held them captive. The United States would have suffered crippling casualties on the road to Tokyo had it not been for the atom bomb, which proved to be a warring world's magic lamp to peace.

It is not without reason that China, even today, labels Japan barbaric, and many would agree with that view. From my own experiences in war-time Malaya and Singapore I can say that, in military jackets, the Japanese take a complete somersault from their normal everyday lives, presenting a most hideous form. The reason for such a mad metamorphosis is to sought in their special relationship with their Emperor, who is considered such a divine manifestation that none dared to even look at his face on the rare occasions that he travelled in his Cadillac or Rolls Royce outside the palace. If anybody happened to be on the roadside at such a rare moment he or she would shut their eyes and turn their face to the ground as the imperial car glides along. You can imagine what frenzy it would create among the people if the military clique were to call the people to arms to preserve *Tenno-Heika*, as happened in 1941. That same frenzy still gripped the Japanese in Malaya. Millions would have gone the way of the McElvies in Selangor in 1942 if the Japanese were provoked in mid-1945. People kept themselves as far away from the Japanese as possible. But those who worked with the Japanese went about their business quietly, scarcely opening their mouths. Even as crowds and pavement stalls blossomed in the evenings all over the country, silence was still an impost on the population. Stories circulated of the disembowelled body of a cabaret girl exhibited in the street of a town upcountry. She was said to have told a bosom friend, a detective, of what befell The Tiger in the Philippines, and she was crow's feed the following morning. There were others whose information carried into the jungle led to the decimation of Japanese contingents that ventured near the Communists' hideouts. Many Malayans looked to the Communists to provide a sanctuary to survive the impending showdown. I know many, mostly Chinese, who fled into the jungle and remained with the Communists until Lord Mountbatten's arrival in Singapore towards the end of the year.

Malays, however, were a little luckier. They were able to retreat to the relative security of their kampongs. They danced the *joget* or played cards and worked the fields to while away the time. They were very self-sufficient, producing their own rice, vegetables and fruits. But with the INA's departure from Burma, Indians had practically nothing to look up to. Some INA men who were landed on the coast of Kerala from Japanese submarines were captured and summarily executed by the British in 1943, but the British did not interfere with the shiploads of Indians from Malaya cast ashore in Madras until August 1947 when liquidation of the British Empire began to take effect. Nor did they, in any way, restrain those who preferred to remain in Malaya after the war.

At the period under review here, the Malayan Railways, hitherto puffing out of stations at a leisurely pace, had been working overtime with a full complement of passengers. Breasts full of tiny tots, old wives were visiting station after station looking for long-lost husbands and sons/daughters. For some it was the journey's end; for others it was the beginning of a new life. Malaya had never known hunger – its nets were full of edible fish or its rubber trees and dredges were earning pound sterling or dollars – but the period of Japanese occupation let down thousands upon thousands. There was acute hunger, but neither the hungry nor the well-fed wants it to be publicized because matter-of-fact Chinese philosophy is those who have eyes would come by food, if not now a few minutes later. By hook or crook, food must be found.

In short, everybody in Malaya at the time was greatly puzzled, or rather in a fit of *mokusatsu* – neither here nor there! Hours slipped by, until all was over. And our poor world had another lease of life.

21

Sayonara

I

SOON AFTER my return to Kuala Lumpur in the last week of May I went for a medical check-up before a Japanese army doctor who soon dispatched me to Fraser's Hill for resumption of my 'convalescence'. He seemed to have detected a faint squeak after every ten beats of my poor heart. Back at the nursing home in the hill station, three Japanese and I were the sole occupants in a 25-bed ward, with half a dozen male nurses and two specialists to attend on us. Unlike my earlier visit to Fraser's Hill in June 1942 when every available inch of habitable space was filled to overflowing with happy and free-and-easy officers, my present sojourn was in a veritable sleepy hollow. Everyone was somehow killing time. And the two specialists hovered around my bed practically throughout the day and wakeful hours of the night, poking me with question after question on the possible direction the war might take. Often I presumed to be suffering from loss of memory due, of course, to the squeak in my heart. I knew it was foolish, even fatal, to open one's mind to a Japanese. But I was ever eager to listen. They again plied me with questions because they knew I was in the top echelon of Domei. Let us assume their names were Dr Ito and Dr Akiyama. Here's a conversation:

Akiyama: Good morning, John-san. How do you think the winds are blowing? You had not been sincere up to this time, always evading vital topics. Let's be frank. (Ito, too, joined in with this remark. I shook hands with them, and sat down, nursing my not-too-soft chin).

Ito: Now, we all know the fate of the Philippines, and of the capture by the Americans of Lt.-Gen Tomoyuki Yamashita. Has MacArthur reduced Okinawa?

The author: I do not know anything more than you do. MacArthur seems to have reduced Corregidor, and General Yamashita was captured by Americans. To be frank with you, I do not know the present position in Okinawa because there is a lot of haziness in reports reaching us. I suppose the hell let loose there ought to make the Americans stop and think. And if they do they are bound to stop there and direct their war potential elsewhere.

Ito: If they had to converge their entire navy for the reduction of a mere coral reef, the Americans may change the course of war to some other area. Here I agree with John-san. We may look for an invasion attempt in our area.

Akiyama: Yes, I think so. Don't you, John-san?

The author: I quite agree with you.

Similarly, practically everybody in Malaya calculated upon a frontal assault upon the country by the British alone or with

Americans. And the time for such a thrust, it was widely believed then, was near at hand. The way to Tokyo then appeared to be too perilous, persuading Americans to look elsewhere for a sudden break-through, possibly together with the British. So we began what appeared to be an endless ordeal of waiting and watching.

Hidden gold and Straits currency passed through the underworld, changed into *whatever* was needed. It was the choicest food and drink that the average Malayan stood in need of. Only butter and margarine were difficult to come by; nearly every other food and drink was available in Chinatown not only in Singapore but in most of the towns of Malaya. You ought to know where to knock for, and have negotiable currency to settle your bill.

By the 15th of July Malayans had lost hopes of ever welcoming back a British army into Malaya. There was a strange, eerie quiet, an uneasiness, all over the country. Meanwhile, I had been discharged from the nursing home and returned to Domei in Kuala Lumpur. News from Tokyo was scant and local Nippon-go scribes were rearranging old newscasts, giving them a topical turn, to issue to local newspapers.

On August 6 came the atomic finale, but we did not know. Four days later – August 10 – we were told not to go home. Strange. Besides me there were 10 local men and women in the KL Domei's English section. We were told not to leave the premises. We were allowed to use the ground floor while about twenty Japanese newsmen lolled on the first floor, drinking like the devil.

Wondering and fearing the worst we waited. Long-drawn-out arguments could be heard from the first floor late into the night when a few of the Japanese tried to get away from it all by resorting to *harakiri*. They were restrained, and all was quiet again.

We were looked after very well – *kopi-o*, bread and fruit for breakfast and rice, vegetables and meat or fish twice a day, but none could have a shave or change of clothes. My sympathies went to the three girls who came out of the ordeal no worse than the men. I don't know how they did it but their well starched and pressed *cheongsams* remained quite unsullied after our six-day confinement.

What happened during that period in 1945 is history. Each of us knew that something epochal had taken place in Tokyo. Domei newscasts were disrupted from August 7 and although working in a Domei office, we were no wiser than the common Malayan as to what exactly had taken place. On the morning of August 16 we were called into the manager's office where a Japanese subordinate told us in halting English: 'We make apo(rr)ogies keeping you in our house. You go home. Do not talk to anyone. Nippon-jin will be absent with you. But you know where going – the Greater East Asia Co-Prosperity Sphere, in spite of Anglo–Americans. *Banzai* to *Tenno-Heika*!'

Our heads were dutifully bent as *Banzai* was called to the Emperor. Collectively thanking the Japanese, we trooped out of the building in single file, with myself at the head. We had to wait for some time on the veranda because our feminine trio had to retire to the closet before the next ordeal of passing through the heavy military cordon thrown round the office a week ago. On the girls' return, our line was re-formed and wended its way to the gate, fifty yards away. Before we emerged from the office, I secretly told everyone in our party to keep his or her head bent until we had passed the military cordon, and not to utter a word about the abrupt end of our service on Domei except in whispered monosyllables to the closest relatives. That is, if they didn't want their heads to be severed as the dawn of peace was about visible.

As we reached the gate, the cordon's commander who was bathed in perspiration thundered an order in Nippon-go and, lo, the cordon presented arms! I was completely dumbfounded and murmured '*Ohayo gozaimasu*' and passed on to the road. Everyone in the party whispered the Japanese greeting and followed me, head still bent and face not reflecting in the least the great fireworks lighting up the dimmest crevices of our inner self. So ended our three-and-a-half years' travail under Japanese occupation.

Mr S Bhaskaran, an old colleague from *The Madras Mail* who was also on the *Malaya Tribune* in Singapore, was the local head of KL Domei's English section. My assignment was with Singapore Domei, having come to Kuala Lumpur only for recuperation. Although a few inches taller and a few pounds heavier than Bhaskaran, I confess I was less resourceful than him. A Chinese staffer among us suggested we have luncheon in a Chinese restaurant before our small party of eleven dispersed. Even the girls plumped for a parting *makan*. I fell in with the idea but Bhaskaran was definitely against it. He said the military situation was most explosive. If the craze for *harakiri* bewitched the Japanese none could say where we would be tomorrow. We all bowed before commonsense, and dispersed quietly to our homes. 'Meet somewhere some day, cheerio!'

The same evening, I packed my troubles and boarded a full train for Singapore which steamed into the station early in the morning of August 17. I walked half a mile from the station with my bag until I could coax a trishaw man to take me to my Middle Road flat for a 50-cent Straits coin (the Railway was still accepting military scrip). From about May, Straits currency was the only legal tender passable in Chinatown and at the time of my arrival in the city it was the only acceptable medium for all private transactions. As none of the conquering army had yet appeared in Malaya the Japanese sought to make hay while the sun still shone by dumping mountains of banana notes. Fortunately few Japanese could take anything worthwhile from Singapore because by the end of the month all had to fall in line at Changi jail prior to being taken to General MacArthur's Japan. What a miracle was the atom! Japanese were at the receiving end then. Aladdin's magic lamp was once again rubbed in the year of grace 1945.

I am not a very demonstrative person. Yet, as I met my brother Jose in front of my flat in Middle Road both of us cried in relief. The war was over, we sensed it. Soon news of the Japanese surrender spread through the city and the mainland. Yet we could not fathom why Mountbatten or MacArthur gave us the go-by. I was agreeably surprised to be called in by an old Chinese friend to help him finish off two bottles of cognac brandy. We leisurely gulped down our '*yamsengs*' to the forget-me-not aroma of 3½-year-old British cigarettes.

II

I DISCOVERED that the city had been shedding the remnants of its 3½-year occupation and donning once again its old, tattered garb of colonialism that was to remain ill-fitting for a generation to come. Old colonial *sahibs*' hill-top bungalows were being refurbished after a lavish bath in phenyls. And they still smelled Japanese, many a newcomer often complained. Workmen were busy trimming hedges, mending swards and filling up pot-holes in garden paths while those *amahs* who survived the occupation returned eagerly to their old havens to de-Nipponise the apartments, all waiting for the old *tuans* and their mems to return.

For weeks the entire population had been sitting back, chewing the cud of over forty months' occupation. How it suddenly came to an end was still a mystery to most. Only few at the time were aware of the first ever atomic-bomb explosions in Japan. But soon the masses became aware that their new-found freedom was entirely due to the Americans and not in the least to the British. Although this is not wholly true, this view found vast adherents in Asian Singapore. That was why the first contingent of British-Indian troops parachuted over Kallang airfield in the third week of August was, at first, dismayed by the city's lukewarm reaction to General Mountbatten and his aides who landed in Kallang the following day. As the people rushed about trying to mend the threads of their existence that were snapped on British surrender in 1942, it also became clear that the apparent sense of being members of the same family that subsisted between Asian races and the British before the war had been lost.

The people had a different reason to be profoundly thankful for: the return to Singapore of company after company of Communist insurgents, mostly Chinese, who had been in the peninsular jungles waging a fruitless war. They trickled back to Singapore, expecting the British to roll out the red carpet for them but were sorely disappointed to be received rather coldly. Nevertheless Chinatown was ablaze with crackers and fireworks as long-lost boys and girls returned to their parents. But the returnees found no joy in British hostility and lack of appreciation for their sacrifices, therefore it was not long before they scampered back into the jungles, and the British had to wage a relentless campaign for nearly ten years until they were weaned out of the jungle.

Among the first batch of British paratroopers to descend on Singapore was an old friend and colleague, Colonel Unni Nair. Way back in the Thirties, Unni and I graduated from the Madras Christian College and joined a British-owned paper there on fifty rupees a month. After eight years of slogging I fled to Singapore and Unni to Delhi where, eventually, his University Training Corps qualification gave him a job in SEAC's information section. As soon as the colonel completed his immediate military tasks he drove right round the city, inquiring where I could be contacted. Eventually, he met me in a friend's home in McNair Road. Tearfully, we celebrated the occasion with canned beer and English cigarettes which the colonel had brought. Five years later he was killed in a jeep accident in Seoul when he visited Korea as a United Nations observer. (It seems his jeep touched a live wire protruding into the road from landmines stacked on the roadside.)

The colonel's meeting with me had been part of his military tasks. He submitted a confidential report to SEAC that absolved me of 'wartime crimes'. A few weeks later, an Englishman called on me to see if the colonel's previous report was correct. I told him I had not gone to Domei for a job but rather it was the other way round. An armed escort had taken me by car to Domei where I was confronted with this poser: 'If you want a job we can give you one; but if the offer is declined, well, it's your choice, not ours.' I preferred to live rather than be disembowelled.

To say that Singapore was not much interested in the British return doesn't mean that the city was sorry for the Japanese. Far from it. For so merciful a redemption from the heavy yoke of occupation all in Singapore as well as other occupied regions knelt before the Creator and offered thanksgiving. For the first time since February 1942 bells tolled in every church, mosque or temple. Those of us who could find time went over to Kallang or the highways leading to Fort Canning for a glimpse of the SEAC commander and his entourage. But the lack of interest in Mountbatten's visit was quite noticeable. Nor did many hang around the roadside as Japanese troops swept the roads and cleaned the drains, as the British prisoners had done in

1942. All the Japanese were soon rounded up all over Malaya and locked up in Changi jail. Then they were all shipped off to Japan.

And every man had to turn a new page in his life. The incessant traffic humming on Singapore's highways day and night today bears irrefutable testimony to the hard and relentless work of the Singaporean, yellow, coffee or white. The man who succeeded me on the old *Malaya Tribune* when I came away to India in 1947, Sinnathamby Rajaratnam, at time of writing Singapore's Foreign Minister and ex-officio delegate to the United Nations.[1] He was always very receptive to my thoughts on independence but at the time we could not see a clear path. There was not even a suitable political party in Singapore.

By the first week of September, Singapore's population had bloated to nearly two million, more than double its prewar numbers. Every hotel from high class to the lowest in Geylang was filled to capacity. Large numbers were searching for long-lost relatives, many of whose bones lay scattered from Rangoon to Hong Kong. Emaciated women, carrying their entire brood with them, could be seen click-clacking on Chinese clogs all over the city, looking for husbands or children. Rarely was a young wife re-united with her husband who, if alive, was perchance still in

---

[1] He was all those things, and went on to be a co-founder of the People's Action Party, became Deputy Prime Minister and remained a Cabinet Minister for many years. Singapore honoured him with the establishment of the S Rajaratnam School of International Studies and the naming of the S Rajaratnam Block at his alma mater, Raffles Institution. He died in 2006 at the age of 91.

the jungle.

My old paper, *The Malaya Tribune*, was revived in September 1945 under my editorship, thanks to Mr Khoo Teng Soon (later Managing Editor of *The Straits Times*) who worked ceaselessly to resume its publication. With the very limited resources at our disposal we produced an eight-page tabloid-size paper until Mr Glover returned from India early the following year. Months before the paper was wound up, I returned to India at the end of 1947.

Epilogue

by Joshua Parapuram

I was five years old when the family entered a dark phase, nervous and sad. The neighbours were moody and edgy. I can remember standing in the driveway of our house and others in Jalan Abdullah in Bangsar, Kuala Lumpur, singing farewell to several families, mostly British colonials, as they packed up and went away for the duration. We sang *Wish me luck as you wave me goodbye*. An older girl who lived three doors away had a twist to the song: *Give me a pie I can eat all the time, In my mouth while I'm eating*.

The good humour did not last. In due course we, too, packed up and departed. The Battle of Britain was raging but we were too young to understand what the adults were whispering about. My father left the family with his father in India and returned to Singapore with his younger brother. Why? Bravado? The Pacific War broke out three weeks after he returned to Singapore. He had two dangerous encounters with drunken Japanese soldiers. In one of these a rifle was swung at him. He had turned his face at the last moment and the blow fell on his back. There was no visible damage but the gun butt had struck him in the head and there was an injury. That eventually led to bouts of amnesia, fatal to the career of a journalist. He has omitted any mention of this in *Sayonara Singapura* although he recounted the incident to his children and grandchildren. Was it a deliberate omission or was amnesia to blame?

When I was 12 and a St Andrew's School student in Singapore, I can remember accompanying my father to the General Hospital in Outram Road. We saw a man sitting behind a desk surrounded by empty shelves. 'See, John,' I remember him saying, 'no medicines, no beds, no nurses. There is nothing. The British are back but nothing else.'

Shortly after that my father handed the reins to Sinnathamby Rajaratnam and left the *Tribune*. He took his family to Calcutta where *The Statesman*, very generously, employed him for about a year. They remembered his wartime broadcasts. We moved south to Madras where in turn he worked for *The Hindu*, the *Express*, the *Madras Mail* and it was while he was at the defunct *Indian Republic* that his amnesia attacks came to a head: he had a stroke that paralysed the left side of his body. He recovered eventually, except for a limp in his left leg, but his working life was effectively over.

In the last chapter he says an Englishman interviewed him in his *Tribune* office about his wartime activities without identifying man. I can relate now that he was Bob Pidgeon, ex-MI5, who sat next to me on *The Straits Times* subbing desk in Kuala Lumpur for many years. He must have known I was John's son. A mutual friend and colleague, the late NTR Singam, told me, relieved to get it off his chest. 'Now I can tell you, Josh,' he told me, the day after Bob died suddenly. He told me that Bob had concluded that no further enquiries were required because India was about to obtain independence. The words Bob used, according to Singam, were, 'It's all purely academic now.' They shook hands and parted. *Kismet* eventually brought Bob and John's son together.

The *Tribune* did not last much longer. Its presses had been dismantled and taken to Indonesia by the Japanese. After the Japanese surrender the machinery was brought back to Singapore and re-assembled, but, like Humpty Dumpty, it could never be put together again. It kept breaking down. Vale, *Tribune*.

My whole family seems to have been born under a wandering star. Following kindergarten at St Paul's, Kuala Lumpur, my schooling continued at All Saints (Trichur, Kerala, India), St Albert's (Ernakulam, Kerala), St Andrew's (Singapore), St Joseph's (Calcutta), St Bede's (Madras) and finishing Year 10 at St John de Britto (Fort Cochin, Kerala). My siblings were similarly afflicted, although the names of the educational establishments differ. What followed is another story.

Joshua Parapuram

Photos

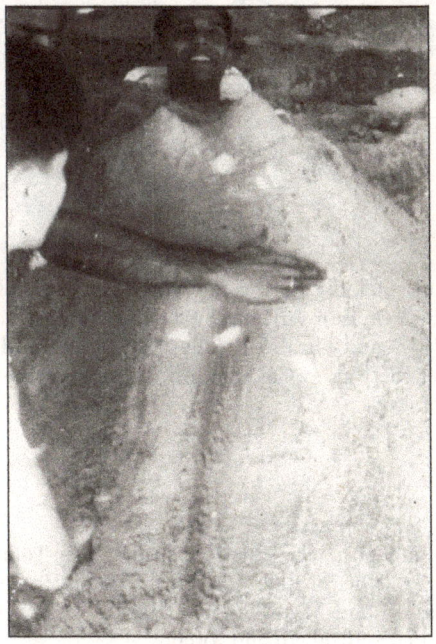

A day at the beach as the storm clouds gathered: Joseph John basking in the sand with his family at Changi beach, not far from where a massacre took place some months later.

The Parapurams in India during the war: Annie (Joseph John's wife, centre) with children, from left, Sarah (Sheila), Joshua (Thampan), eldest child Joseph (Joy) and Elizabeth (Jolly). The youngest, Usha, was not born until after the war, in Calcutta. All the others were better known by their pet-names.

Return to Singapore after the war: Joseph John (standing left) with Annie and his brother Jose, with friends Tom Thaddeus (holding Sarah) and Mrs Thaddeus (back). The other children are Joshua (left), Elizabeth and Joseph.

Growing up in India: Joy with Usha, Sheila and Jolly. Thampan went to Singapore in 1953 at the age of 17 and became a reporter in *The Straits Times*. Joy became a train driver in India, and the girls all became teachers.

Early days at the *Tribune*: Morning news conference shortly after Joseph John (far left) arrived as leader writer. Others, from his left, are Sub-editor Charlie Tamboe, Assistant Editor G.S. Hammond, then Editor Edwin Maurice Glover, News Editor Lim Keng Hor, Features Editor F.A. Love (partly hidden), Advertising Manager Mrs F. Retz and Sub-editor S.T. Keong.

Party time at the *Domei* news agency while the war raged in the Pacific: Joseph John has manoeuvred himself into an insignificant position for the group picture. He is last man standing on the left.

Another anniversary party at the *Domei*: The war was going well for the Japanese, and there was plenty of liquor, but just to remind everyone of the true nature of their presence in Singapore a Samurai sword is on display in front. Joseph John has again manoeuvred himself into an insignificant position second from the right at the back.

The censored *Book of Common Prayer*. Many lines and many pages of religious books used by prisoners in the Changi concentration camp were blacked out. The stupidity of the act is self-evident.

Gathering of survivors: Staff of the late great *Malaya Tribune* shortly after its second coming following the war, with the Editor, Parapuram Joseph John (front row, centre), with T.S. Khoo (Chief Sub, on his right) and Edwin Maurice Glover (now Managing Editor, on his left).

The final goodbye to Singapore: Joseph John with Thampan and Sheila (married and living in Singapore). When this picture was taken Joseph John was carrying a limp in his left leg following a stroke that ended his working career.

The fall of Malaya and Singapore

You'll Die in Singapore
9789814625562

Malayan Spymaster
9789810854423

Out in the Midday Sun
9789814625319

Our Man in Malaya
9789814423861

The Defence and Fall of Singapore
9789814423885

The Boat
9789810583019